The Origin of Cultures

How Individual Choices
Make Cultures Change

W. Penn Handwerker

Left
Coast
Press
Inc.

Walnut Creek, CA

**Left
Coast
Press**
Inc.

Left Coast Press, Inc.
1630 North Main Street, #400
Walnut Creek, California 94596
http://www.LCoastPress.com

Hardback ISBN 978-1-59874-067-7
Paperback ISBN 978-1-59874-068-4

Library of Congress Cataloging-in-Publication Data
Handwerker, W. Penn.
  The origin of cultures : how individual choices make cultures change / W. Penn Handwerker.
      p. cm.— (Key questions in anthropology)
ISBN 978-1-59874-067-7 (hardcover : alk. paper) — ISBN 978-1-59874-068-4 (pbk. : alk. paper)
1. Culture—Origin. I. Title.
    GN357.5.H36 2009
    306—dc22
                              2009028843
09 10 11 12 5 4 3 2 1

Printed in the United States of America
∞™ The paper used in this publication meets the minimum requirements of American National Standard for Information Sciences—Permanence of Paper for Printed Library Materials, ANSI/NISO Z39.48—1992.

Cover design by Hannah Jennings

The Origin of Cultures

Key Questions in Anthropology: Little Books on Big Ideas

Series Editor: H. Russell Bernard

Key Questions in Anthropology are small books on large topics. Each of the distinguished authors summarizes one of the key debates in the field briefly, comprehensively, and in a style accessible to college undergraduates. Anthropology's enduring questions and perennial debates are addressed here in a fashion that is both authoritative and conducive to fostering class debate, research, and writing. Proposals for books in the series should be addressed to ufruss@ufl.edu

Series Editor H. Russell Bernard (emeritus, University of Florida), has been editor of the journals *American Anthropologist, Human Organization,* and *Field Methods,* and of the series Frontiers of Anthropology. He is author of the leading textbook on field methods and has published extensively in cultural, applied, and linguistic anthropology. He is recipient of the prestigious AAA Franz Boas Award.

Series Titles

Archaeology Matters: Action Archaeology in the Modern World
    Jeremy A. Sabloff

The Origin of Cultures: How Individual Choices Make Cultures Change
    W. Penn Handwerker

Contents

Preface

I've been working on this book since 1962, my freshman year at Willamette University. I haven't finished it yet, but I think this formulation is worth sharing. Inside, you'll find an incipient theory of how much of the living (albeit primarily human) world works. This theory proposes mechanisms that integrate multiple phenomenal levels (genes, cells, central nervous systems, individual organisms, and populations) and emergent phenomena like ideas, choices, social relations, and cultures. Their operation explains where new cultural things come from and how they become concentrated in the collective agreements and patterned behavior we call cultures. By accounting for the origin of cultures, we also account for both the minutia and the broad sweep of human history.

Russ Bernard invited me to write this book. I appreciate the opportunity. I hope the outcome repays partially his kindnesses over nearly 40 years of friendship. I owe much to Rose Jones and Roy D'Andrade. Rose insisted that I treat cultures seriously. Roy pointed out that cultures really can do things. He then left the observation sitting there for me to figure out how, exactly, and to work out some of the implications. Victor Davis Hanson's *Carnage & Culture* showed me how to effectively frame some of those implications. Nearly 30 years ago, Eric Wolf's *Europe and the People without History* urged us to stop thinking of cultures as bounded wholes and identify the processes by which cultures come into being, evolve, and disappear. In *Carnage & Culture,* Hanson asks us to consider the possibility that the specific configurations of different cultures constitute designs which, with varying degrees of success, accomplish goals. This means that thinking of cultures as teams isn't just a metaphor and implies the operation of selective mechanisms at multiple levels, from individuals to cultures. Determining how resiliency may emerge from specific configurations of cultural stuff will teach us how we may effectively evolve cultural institutions that promote sustainability. It will simultaneously give substance to Kroeber's vision of cultures as superorganic entities.

Catherine Fuentes tried to tell me all this much earlier but I didn't listen well—I apologize, Cat: you were right and I was wrong. Schaun Wheeler wrote a wonderful dissertation called *Everything We Don't Know About People: An Argument for a Justifiable, Useful, and Respectable Social Science, with Illustrations from a Small, Central Asian Country.* He takes some of the ideas presented here further and takes issue with others. I received his manuscript too late to incorporate it into this book in ways that I'd like. But I urge everyone to read it.

Dan Adler, Alan Ballew, Bob Bee, Russ Bernard, Nicola Bulled, Darrell and Joy Champion, Lance Crooks, Stuart Miller, and Natalie Munro helped me improve my writing and my presentation. Many thanks! Since I didn't always take their good advice, don't blame them for what you don't like. If you find the reading easy, though, thank Martha Ward.

While I struggled to finish this manuscript, Joanie cared for me and made my life incredibly interesting, in extraordinarily positive ways. This one is for her.

CHAPTER ONE

The Puzzle

This book explains where new cultural things come from and how they become concentrated in the collective agreements and patterned behavior we call cultures. The answers will help you understand otherwise senseless events, like why Ayat al-Akhras detonated the bomb she had wrapped around her body to murder Rachel Levy.

The fact that both girls were about the same age (17, 18) captured media attention for a day or two. Less interesting was that the bomb that Ayat set off in Jerusalem's Kiryat Yovel supermarket also killed the guard who stopped her near the door and wounded twenty-eight other shoppers. After all, this was only one of 108 terrorist attacks in Israel in 2002, and it only killed two people. The Khobar Towers bombing in Saudia Arabia in 1996 had killed ten times this number. The U.S. Embassy bombings in Kenya and Tanzania in 1998 killed more than ten times the number of people killed in the Khobar Towers bombing. The attacks on the United States on September 11, 2001, killed significantly more than ten times the number of people killed in the U.S. Embassy bombings, three orders of magnitude greater than the deaths at the Kiryat Yovel supermarket.

In the mid-20th century, terrorist incidents reported in the international media numbered one or two per year. The number rose to around one per day through the late 20th century. Terrorist incidents skyrocketed to around three per day by the first years of the 21st century. The attack that killed Rachel Levy constituted only one of the 760 terror attacks on Israel carried out after the signing of the Oslo agreement in 1993, which was intended to establish nonviolent relations between Israel and Palestinians. Rachel Levy died in Israel. But jihadist terrorist attacks have also killed Russians, Americans, British, Danes, Canadians, Saudis, Germans, French, Egyptians, Jordanians, Indians, Australians, Japanese, Filipinos, Indonesians, Pakistanis, Iraqis, and

Afghanis. Jihadists left Dutch filmmaker Theo van Gogh dead on the sidewalk with a knife in his chest and the editor of a Sudanese newspaper, Mohammed Taha, without a head. Jihadist threats drove Hirsi Ali, a member of the Dutch parliament, to flee to the United States, and they caused Seyran Ates, a German women's rights lawyer who won the Berlin Women's Prize in 2004 and a Civil Courage Prize in 2005, to close her law practice. Over the last 3 years, jihadists have carried out more than 700 attacks in southern Thailand. The Rand-MIPT database now contains information on nearly 31,000 terrorist attacks carried out since 1968.

Why would a girl kill herself to murder people who she did not know and had done her no harm? If she felt impelled to kill, why not learn to shoot a rifle and kill soldiers at a distance? But why did she kill—why not write to the newspaper or hold a nonviolent protest? Why not complete her secondary schooling, complete college, get an MBA, and start a business that manufactured farm implements or household furniture to raise her compatriots' standard of living, and help transform Palestine into a prosperous, independent state?

Quick answers don't get to the heart of the matter. The heart of the matter is that Ayat did not act alone, and the elements that went into her behavior may be traced to a striking array of places and times, including ancient Jewish thought in the 3rd millennium BC, China in the 8th century, and Bell Labs in the 20th. How did they originate? What happened for them to get from their origins to concentrate in Ayat's mind and behavior?

And not only Ayat's mind and behavior—large numbers of people throughout the world risk their lives, or kill themselves, to participate in a global jihadic culture by murdering people they do not know and who did them no harm. They don't write letters to newspapers. They don't hold peaceful protests. They don't start businesses that produce food or household furniture. Like all cultures, this one consists of patterned behavior and a coordinated set of activities (involving recruitment, training, supplies, financing, target selection, insertion, detonation, and advertisement), which its participants rationalize with a set of shared norms, which derive from shared assumptions about the things that make up the world of experience. Sayyid Qutb and, later, Ayman Muhammad Rabi' Al-Zawahiri, made explicit the most important of the assumptions that rationalize jihad:

The Origin of Cultures

- Allah constitutes the highest authority for human affairs;

- Shari'a, based primarily on the word of Allah (the *Qur'an*) and the practices of the Prophet Muhammad, constitutes the ultimate law for all humans;

- apostasy consists of any rejection of the first two principles and constitutes a crime punishable by death;

- Muslims who reject the first two principles, any non-Muslim who rejects Islam by failing to convert, and democracies, because they assume that the people who are governed constitute the ultimate authority for human affairs, count as examples of apostasy.

The norms of jihadic behavior follow from these assumptions:

- democracies should be destroyed; and

- all individuals guilty of apostasy, Muslim or non-Muslim, should be killed.

The cultural inviolability of the central assumptions about Allah and Shari'a, the definition of apostasy, its association with the death penalty, and what counts as apostasy vary dramatically from one time and place to another and within any given region at a particular time. Jihadic culture adherents generally consider Saudi Arabia an apostate, for example, despite its application of Shari'a, which has been so rigid that its religious police refused to let schoolgirls flee a burning building because they were insufficiently covered. By contrast, the *Newsweek* story of Ayat's murder-suicide by Joshua Hammer reported that her fiancé said that he would have stopped her if he had known ahead of time and hoped that God would forgive her—the *Qur'an* condemns both homicide and suicide as sins. Although jihadists joyfully advertised her death, Ayat's father voiced the intense pain that parents endure with the death of a child.

Muslims ordinarily don't think and act very differently from ordinary Hindus, Buddhists, Christians, or Jews. And, in that, we glimpse the shared humanity that produces cultural similarities and, sometimes, dramatic cultural differences, by concentrating in one shared set of understandings and coordinated activities things that originated at many different places and times.

This book will show that the cultural processes that explain Ayat's murder of Rachel also explain why Rachel went to the supermarket. It will also show that the processes that led Ayat to murder Rachel operate independently of Islam, Christianity, or Judaism and result at other times and places in 62 million people murdered in the U.S.S.R. between 1917 and 1987, genocides in the Balkans, Rwanda, and Darfur, and the battering and death of women and children worldwide. The processes that explain mass murder also explain cultural resiliency and come unbidden from people born, just like you and me, with minds that think creatively and respond predictably to variation in the consequences of choices.

This book focuses on the evolution of human choices. Here's one central finding: Human imagination consistently produces new things as well as new ways of thinking about old things that radically change the options from which we may choose. We confidently predict unpredictability—that we cannot perfectly predict the choices any one person will make. We thus can't tell you precisely why Ayat, but not her school friends, fiancé, or parents, chose to kill herself. We also cannot foretell the future effectively.

Here's another central finding: Consequences matter. We thus confidently predict predictable effects of specific kinds of consequences. When people choose to kill themselves, suicide must not produce consequences that compare badly with the consequences of making a different choice. Given the time and circumstances of her birth and upbringing, this probably held true for Ayat.

Cultures originate out of the choices individuals make within the bounds of their specific experiential history. The criteria by which people make these choices explain the origins and evolution of specific cultures. They also suggest what it may take to effectively address contemporary policy questions—like how we can:

+ reduce the likelihood of terrorist acts;

+ effectively respond to a global avian flu epidemic;

+ improve the health and material well-being of people throughout the world;

+ maintain or increase energy supplies; or

+ deal with fundamental climate change.

You'll need some background to understand how and why mechanisms in the minds with which you and I were born create cultures and change them. Chapter 2 will explain where new cultural things come from and how the Islam of Ayat evolved out of Christianity and the Judaism of Rachel. In the process, it will explain:

◆ why new things must come from old things;

◆ why the things of the moment set limits on the future;

◆ why individuals can't help but create new things;

◆ why each of us is unique and can't be otherwise;

◆ why we all make mistakes all the time; and

◆ why we can't predict the future.

Chapter 3 will outline the principal patterns of cultural evolution that emerge from the ways in which minds take information from sensory fields and produce cultural outputs. These include why the contemporary jihadic culture that captured Ayat, like all cultures, consists of things created at other times in other places and why Ayat murdered Rachel in a supermarket. In the process, it will explain:

◆ how and why people with no contact invent the same things;

◆ how and why cultures evolve divergently;

◆ how many cultures may contribute to the evolution of a single cultural synthesis;

◆ how and why cultural diversity in today's world emerged from periods of isolation and later information flow;

◆ why information volume regulates how much we learn from our neighbors, which makes enclaved cultures evolve in different directions than the cultures that surround them; but

◆ that the utility of information regulates *what* we learn.

Chapter 4 will explain why we act on useful information and what makes something useful or not. In the process, it will explain how living in fear that your father, uncles, or brothers may kill you, as Ayat probably did, changes how you look at the prospect of killing yourself. Thus, it will explain:

◆ why people learn some things but not others;

- why people weigh costs and benefits;

- why never "looking death in the eye" promotes fantasy;

- why winnowing makes cultures look, in retrospect, like they were purposefully designed to minimize energy expenditure and maximize energy capture;

- why human culture history exhibits directional change toward increasing levels of productivity; and

- why the most consistent producers of cultural evolution are climate change, population change, and the human exercise of power.

Chapter 5 will examine how specific variation in consequences produces specific forms of cultural evolution and establish a framework for better characterizing the cultural clashes that led Ayat to murder Rachel. In the process, it will explain:

- how and why climate change, population change, and human behavior dictate our choices;

- why Lord Acton was right;

- why Sun Tzu, Machiavelli, and Beccharia were right; and

- what this means for the direction of cultural evolution.

Chapter 6 will look at lessons learned and will end where it began, with Rachel, Ayat, and a jihad against Western culture solely dependent on that culture for whatever success it may achieve. In the process, it will explain:

- how our minds formulate and select among choice options;

- what democratic Japan has in common with the Bowl Championship Series;

- why religions, like guns, don't kill unless someone pulls the trigger; and

- why the cultural assumption that each person knows best may produce the most resilient cultures.

First, however, let's look more closely at this thing we call culture. Culture takes on different meanings, depending on how you look at it, and a satisfactory account must explain important features of each view. Most important, this book will account for both ideas and behavior and explain why and how they come to correspond fairly closely, but never close to perfectly. It will also account for our ancestors' proclivity for doing things better and better, and why doing things better meant creating qualitatively different ways of living as our ancestors shifted from simple hunting and gathering to food production to free-market industrial production. I will explain how some cultures acquire names and others don't, how each of us participates in many cultures, some of which extend around the globe, and how and under what circumstances cultures either change or remain the same. But the underlying issue concerns human minds and how they work to learn some things but not others.

What's This Thing Culture?

In his 1871 book *Primitive Culture*, Edward B. Tylor wrote that culture consists of "that complex whole which includes knowledge, belief, art, morals, law, custom, and any other capabilities and habits acquired by man as a member of society" (p. 1). Tylor thus provided anthropology its first modern definition of culture. He made two important observations. First, culture is a holistic, integrated thing. Culture isn't just art, or families, or ways of making a living, or religion. Culture is all of these and more because the things that comprise it fit together. Second, we acquire it by virtue of living with other people—we *learn* our cultures.

Alfred Kroeber and Clyde Kluckhohn published a comprehensive review of uses of the term culture in 1952. They found a consensus about this acquired, holistic thing that focused Tylor's enumerative definition more tightly. "Culture," they wrote, "consists of patterns, explicit and implicit, of and for behavior, . . . including their embodiments in artifacts" (1952:181).

Over the last half of the 20th century, anthropologists used the word culture to refer to an array of things. Marvin Harris and a small number of other cultural anthropologists, along with most archaeologists and biological anthropologists, continued to write about culture as something that encompassed both ideas and behavior. Archaeologists, of course, work primarily with the embodiment in artifacts of "patterns of and for behavior," material culture. In the late

1950s and 1960s, the anthropologist Ward Goodenough argued that the most useful definition of culture was the one that restricted it to shared ways of thinking about the world. Cognitive anthropologists like Roy D'Andrade systematically examined the structure, organization, and operation of culture as a shared set of ideas. By the end of the 20th century, most cultural anthropologists had adopted this narrower view of culture. I did, too, for most of my career. However, over the past few years I've come to think of a culture as a (more-or-less) coherent set of patterned and coordinated activities rationalized by a shared set of norms, which are rationalized by a shared set of assumptions about the world of experience. I place emphasis on behavior rather than ideas because behavior provides the information our minds use to produce behavior, and what we do or don't do determines how well, or if, we live.

Directional Change in Productivity

Culture, too, means different things depending on the level of comparison we use. If we focus on ourselves as individuals, it's plain that each of us constitutes a unique being. If we focus on ourselves as fellow members of the same biological group, *Homo sapiens*, we see similarities that dramatically set us and our ancestors apart from other living things. A survey of our shared history over the last 300,000 years or so, for example, reveals dramatic growth in productivity, the number and kind of cultural elements, and the complexity of their organization. In the middle Stone Age, our ancestors made a living by foraging—hunting game and gathering plants. Initially, they used simple, partially flaked stone cobbles, stones that had been carefully and fully chipped to resemble a flattened, pear-shaped oval with a sharp edge around most of the circumference, called hand-axes, sharp blades that had been carefully removed from fine-grained stone cores, grindstones, and pigments. Over time, they added small, sharp stone points and they developed techniques for shell fishing, long-distance trade, fishing, mining, and means to make tools out of bone, including barbed points. By the beginning of the late Stone Age, they made a wide variety of tools with very small shaped stones called microliths and made beads and drew images. Soon afterward, our ancestors added to their material inventory polished stone tools, basketry, nets, weirs, storage techniques and implements, sleds and canoes, bows and arrows, pottery, and domesticated dogs. Despite birth and death rates that produced very, very slow population growth rates (on the order of .001% per year), our foraging ancestors populated Africa by 100,000 years ago, Asia by 50–60,000 years ago, Europe by 40,000 years ago, Indonesia, the Philippines, and Australia by 40,000 years ago, and the Americas perhaps as early as 35,000 years ago.

About 10,000 years ago in East Asia, Southeast Asia, South Asia, Southwest Asia, East Africa, West Africa, North America, Mesoamerica, and South America, specific foraging populations ushered in the agricultural revolution when they transformed themselves into farmers. Farming and farmers spread from Southwest Asia into Europe; from a point of origin in West Africa throughout that region and south across the Congo River basin into the grasslands of central and southern Africa; from an origin in northeast Africa south into the grasslands of East Africa; from a point of origin in what today is central Mexico both north and south; and from the other centers of crop domestication to adjacent regions. Farming spread both because some foragers adopted the new technologies, and because others were killed or driven from their homes. Early farming techniques worked poorly in the drier regions of sub-Saharan Africa, Southwest Asia, and the Central Asian grassland. There, people found ways to make a living off herds of animals—cattle, goats, sheep, camels, and horses, depending on location.

Dramatic population growth in early farming populations led to increasingly productive farming technologies, fighting produced centralized governments and, beginning about 6,000 years ago, metallurgy (in Southwest Asia, the west-central coast of South America, Mesoamerica, and around the Great Lakes and Northwest Coast of North America). About 5,000 years ago, further expansion created the earliest cities and civilizations in the Nile River delta, Mesopotamia, the Indus River Valley, the Yellow River basin, the Valley of Mexico, and the west-central coast of South America in what is now Peru. Life in these earliest civilizations was marked by very high levels of occupational specialization, increasingly complex and sharply stratified social communities, slavery, writing, monumental architecture, major increases in productivity in the form of irrigation-agriculture, money-based exchange, and increasingly important long-distance trade. By the time of the Roman Empire, for example, merchants of the Silk Road moved goods from China to Europe, from which they found their way to the Briton barbarians who lived off the northwestern coast of Europe. In exchange for salt from the Sahara, the forested regions of West Africa sent gold north and provided most of Europe's supply from Roman times on. Malagueta pepper, whose center of supply in historical times was the lightly populated central coast (the Pepper Coast) of what is now Liberia, was carried to northwestern Europe through the trans-Saharan trade by the early 1200s if not earlier.

Just over 200 years ago, the agricultural population in England ushered in the Industrial Revolution when they transformed themselves into manufacturers who employed energy based on steam, electricity, and petroleum in addition to that of people or animals. Industrialization and free markets raised human productivity by several orders of magnitude, generated increasing levels of global competition among increasingly large manufacturing, distribution, and service organizations, broke barriers to communication, trade, and movement, raised standards of living, reduced death rates and birth rates, and both reduced and changed the nature of social inequalities. Today, you can watch the movie *Out of Africa* on a VCR in an African bush village 150 miles from the coast and a 3-hour walk from the nearest road and talk with your broker in London on a cell phone while he tours the British Museum exhibit on ancient Egyptian civilization. After that, you can arrange a flight to Singapore for the following day.

Revolutions Produce Qualitative Change

When we compare people with people, it makes more sense to talk about cultures with reference to shared similarities and dissimilarities rather than the Tylorean "all things that we do and think." Both the Agricultural Revolution and Industrial Revolution ushered in qualitative changes in how people thought and lived their lives. Foragers, for example, tended to live in small, mobile, family-based groups widely spread over space. Whether they lived in the dry Kalahari region of southern Africa, the Australian outback, the rainforest of the Congo, Arctic America, or the grasslands of East Africa, people who made their living hunting game, gathering plant food, and fishing, rarely lived in groups larger than thirty to forty people. Sometimes, foragers collected in numbers as large as 500 or 1,000, but rarely for long periods. Camps of thirty people often broke up into tiny groups of three to ten people, depending on the season.

Camp composition varied widely because foragers had few rules that constrained membership; children characteristically had to find mates in camps other than the one in which they grew up; newly married couples might shift from the camp of the husband's parents to that of the wife's parents; and local droughts, floods, or other conditions that reduced the availability of the wild foods on which life depended might force families, if not entire camps, to move elsewhere. Foragers assumed, like we do, that your family consisted of all people to whom you can trace relationships through both father and mother, bilaterally. Social relations among members of a camp of foragers generally exhibited little inequality and much sharing.

Pastoralists, whether sheep-herding Kazaks of the Central Asian Steppes, camel-herding Bedouin in the Arabian Peninsula, or cattle-herding Fulani, Karimojong, Jie, or Maasai in the sub-Saharan and East African grasslands, tended, like foragers, to live in small, mobile, family-based groups widely spread over the landscape. But pastoral camps tended to consist of a core group of related men and their families organized into family corporations that held title to herds of animals. Each small family corporation traced its descent to earlier ancestors and, through these ancestors, to other small family corporations, and to earlier and earlier ancestors and more distantly related family corporations. The identity of these earliest ancestors lost in the mists of time were replaced by significant beings—perhaps a wolf, or Adam. Thus anchored, ties of ancestry and descent led to living descendants and created bonds between people who lived in widely separated camps, who never met each other until, or if, those bonds were activated for coordinated action. This mode of tracing one's family through patrilineal links, called a system of segmentary lineages, might encompass hundreds of thousands of people, unlike the bilateral linkages between individual foragers that might join together only thirty to forty people through a genealogy of only three to four generations depth.

Among pastoralists, a woman generally had to leave the camp in which she grew up to move to the camp of her new husband and his relatives. Her leaving reduced the family by one worker but brought with it a compensatory gift of cattle, goats, sheep, or camels, as appropriate. The one exception, first described for the ancient Jews in *Numbers* 36:8–9, and still characteristic of Middle Eastern peoples, assigns preferential marriage between the sons and daughters of brothers. Marriage between the children of brothers (meaning, usually, men who belong to the same patrilineal family) keeps both the wealth and manpower within the family. Inequality marked the relations between men and women in pastoralist communities and, to some extent, old and young men. Men owned the herds, defended them when necessary, and enlarged them when they could. Young men depended on their fathers for the basis of their herds, but their fathers depended on sons to manage their herds. Women managed the household and produced the children. If one woman performed poorly, she could be replaced far more easily than a man.

The earliest farmers consisted of small, family units that applied hoes, digging sticks, axes, knives, and sickles to small amounts of land to feed themselves and their families. Farming meant that you found some arable land (perhaps an acre per person), cleared the brush and forest to produce an open area in which to plant crops, called a "swidden," burned the debris to release nutrients back into the soil, planted crops, engaged in practices to minimize weed growth and protect the growing food from birds, rodents, and deer, harvested the mature crop, and stored it for the coming year. Farmers grew two or three starchy staples. In wet regions, this meant rice, or root crops like manioc, yams, and sweet potatoes; in dry regions, it meant grains like millet, sorghum, wheat, and barley. Farmers also grew a dozen or more additional vegetables and fruits and hunted, fished, and collected wild plants, depending on the demands of farming and the relative abundance of these additional sources of food.

Swidden cultivation practices of this kind still prevail in Africa, the Americas, and sporadic locations across Southeast Asia and the islands of the Pacific Basin. This form of agriculture made children very important because the number of people who worked on your farm determined how much food you produced. But plows appeared in Southwest Asia by about 8,000 years ago and were carried throughout Eurasia by 5,000 years ago. Heavy plows with a coulter to cut turf and a mouldboard appeared around 1,400 years ago. About 200 years later, the two-field Mediterranean pattern of alternating a winter crop with fallow was replaced in Northern Europe by the three-field system that alternated a winter crop, fallow, and a spring crop.

Farm settlements might consist of fifty people, or 1,000, 10,000, or 100,000. Small villages might consist, like pastoralist camps, of a core group of related men and their families, although a few (primarily in northeastern North America and central Africa) consisted of a core group of related women and their families. Some communities (scattered primarily along the West African coast) organized themselves into both patrilineal and matrilineal families, and a few (primarily in the Pacific Basin and Indonesia) organized themselves into family corporations defined bilaterally. Individual households consisted of a core set of parents and their children. Although means of birth control and abortion came to be widely known in this preindustrial world, people rarely used them. Except in Europe, where marriage took place relatively late (in women's 20s), women bore children beginning in their teens. In all farming communities, women bore children often, on average experiencing anywhere from six to ten live births by the end of their reproductive years. Child-bearing gave women an importance they did not otherwise enjoy, and women with many children lived far better than women with few. Characteristically, one out of four children born died before they reached their first birthday, and disease or famine might make that three of four children born during hard times. Farmers commonly experienced a life expectancy at birth of only 25 years. This did not mean that everyone died early. Although some reached age 80 or 90, farming communities contained very few elders and they were valued highly.

Marriage meant a process, not a simple ceremony. The process might begin in childhood and it often ended well after the birth of the first children. Over most of the world, the process was marked by gifts given to the family of the bride by the family of the groom and, frequently, work carried out by the groom for his prospective in-laws. Some young men made preferential marriages with their mother's brother's daughter. Others acquired a wife from their father's best friend. In most farming communities, men could marry more than one woman at the same time, a practice called polygyny. Rich, powerful men might have hundreds of wives. In a small region of the Himalayas, women could marry more than one man at the same time, a practice called polyandry. Among Eurasian populations with plow agriculture, which placed a premium on men's knowledge of animal husbandry, families of unmarried daughters provided gifts (a dowry) to the families of prospective sons-in-law.

Commonly, living units of husbands, wives, and their children also included additional relatives who helped with household and farm chores. Extended households might include a young brother or sister of the wife or husband, or the parents of one or both, or a set of brothers and their families, or a set of sisters and their families. Individual households often worked with their neighbors to accomplish farm tasks and shared their food with family, friends, and community members. In larger settlements, these groups of relatives tended to occupy specific regions or quarters of the town or city. In 1850, the Yoruba city of Ibadan counted 100,000 occupants and was ruled by an elaborate administrative bureaucracy but still was divided into quarters, each occupied by the large kinship groups that organized most social relations. Remains that date to around 2,000 years ago from the city of Teotihuacan in the Valley of Mexico, which may have been larger than Rome at the time, show evidence of a similar manner of organization. Farmers who lived as parts of centralized societies with chiefs, or kings, supported the administrative bureaucracy with labor and crops.

Even in the smallest farming communities, inequality marked the relations between old and young and men and women. Younger men depended on the older men who either owned the land or, in communities organized into matrilineal families, managed land allocation. As in pastoral communities, for the most part women managed the household and produced the children. But if one woman performed poorly, she could be replaced. In parts of Africa, a barren wife or a wife who produced many children who died soon after birth might be suspected of witchcraft. Childless women suffered badly compared to others, unless they found a way to foster children from fruitful marriages. The emergence of centralized polities added further inequalities. Some reflected growing occupational specializations (e.g., manufacturers, merchants, service providers, and members of a judiciary and its associated police). The emergence of the institution of slavery and the growing wealth of the king or emperor and religious and political elites produced the most dramatic inequalities.

As recently as the mid-20th century, most Americans lived on farms. Today, only 1% or 2% do, and these few feed much of the world. Among foragers, high birth and death rates meant that children made up much of the population and that perhaps fifteen people fed a camp of thirty. Now, agricultural technologies make it possible for one person to feed 200. The other 199 extract other resources, manufacture things, and transport resources to manufacturers and farmers and both food and manufactured goods to distributors who sell to distributors who sell to consumers who purchase a huge range of services from governmental and nongovernmental organizations, which range from fast-food meals and utilities maintenance and repair to health care, public safety, and national defense. Our move from the land to the cities transformed them. The cities of today dwarf the largest of preindustrialized cities like Rome or Teotihuacan. Nearly 3 million people now live in Rome, and nearly 9 million people now live near Teotihuacan in Mexico City.

Rather than carry wood and water, wash clothes, tend fires, care for animals or accompany a parent to the farm, children in the industrialized world go to school. They know little about what it takes to produce their food supply or move it to local markets. They and their parents hope for a degree from school that will help them acquire well-paying employment from one or more of millions of employers in sectors other than agriculture. The largest single employer, government, consists of a huge bureaucracy concerned with housing, natural resources, transportation, national defense, police, education, unemployment, public safety, and health. Some children grow up in ghettoized neighborhoods and see few opportunities beyond serving as merchants of illicit drugs or other equivalent activities. Furthermore, the industrialized world brought unemployment, which was unknown earlier. Nonetheless, the prevailing goal is to acquire a good job, periodic promotions and pay increases, a lifetime of increasing material welfare, and a leisured old age.

Irrespective of how we end up making a living, we expect to choose our own mates and live where we want, perhaps thousands of miles from our parents and siblings (although sometimes for short periods of time with our parents). We expect to travel, take vacations, watch (color, HD) TV, receive quality health care, cool our house in the summer with an air conditioner, and surf the Web. In the meanwhile, we expect to have no more than two children, if we have any at all. Despite life expectancies at birth that range into the mid 80s in many industrialized countries, we don't produce enough children to replace ourselves. Below-replacement fertility dramatically changed the social landscape. Populations no longer grow without migration, and immigrants rapidly change the composition of populations in ways that threaten native populations. Growth in the proportion of elderly dramatically changed the composition of the labor force, consumer interests and spending habits, and our health care needs. Today, elders in America rarely die at home surrounded by sons, daughters, and grandchildren. Far more likely, they die surrounded by other elders in planned retirement communities and nursing homes.

Names Aren't Cultures

When we make finer comparisons among people, culture often means how specific groups of people live. We learned about foragers, pastoralists, farmers, and the changes wrought by industrialization by studying historical records, by excavating the remains left by former populations, and by living among, observing, and talking with our contemporaries. We differentiated among our contemporaries based on shared similarities and dissimilarities in location, language, and ways of living, called each a culture, and gave each a name, like Nuer, Grebo, Chinese, Arabs, Comanche, Eskimo, or Apache.

Names are tricky things. Sometimes, these names came from enemies of the people we studied. Comanche, for example, originated as a Ute word for "people who want to fight me all the time." Eskimo originated as an Algonkian word for "eaters of raw meat." Apache means "enemy" in Zuni. Sometimes, names of peoples came from major errors of the observer. Columbus, for example, thought that he had

The Origin of Cultures

reached India when he called the people of the New World Indians. Sometimes, names came from the work people did or the manner in which we learned of a group. The Kru of West Africa appear to have acquired their name after, and because, they actively sought work on ships that plied the West African coast in the 1800s. Chinese emerged as an Anglicized version of the name used in trade of an early Chinese dynasty (Chin). All names gloss over internal differences. Chinese, for example, ignores the differences among the more than fifty different national identities or ethnic groups who make up the nearly 1.5 billion people within China's national boundaries. Even Bajan, which applies to fewer than 400,000 people who grew up on Barbados, an island only 15 miles wide by 25 miles long, ignores differences that distinguish people from different parishes.

Scholarly usage over the last century made it easy to imagine that each named culture constituted a distinct thing. As the anthropologist Eric Wolf reminded us in 1982, however, the constituency of such groups, their labels, and even their existence change dramatically. Germans did not exist, for example, until the German Empire melded together dozens of previously independent towns and principalities in 1871. Some of the people we take to be French today were English in the 11th century—or, because England did not exist and the people who lived there had moved from Scandinavia, the people of Normandy were, at that time, as English as anyone could be said to be. Great Britain, formed by Anglo-Saxon domination of native Celtic-speakers, still experiences difficulty with Wales and Scotland. In the summer of 2006, the Scottish National Liberation Army, for example, threatened to poison English water supplies. On the Pepper Coast of West Africa, men who differentiated themselves as father and son became undifferentiated members of a regional political group called a *dako* that competed with its neighbors for control over land, rights over women and children, and trade; men of competing *dako* became undifferentiated "Kru" when they sought work on ships plying the commercial shipping lanes off the West African coast. A few Kru, along with Yoruba and despite marked differences in language, customs, and physical attributes, became undifferentiated slaves who worked plantations in the West Indies and the southern United States. Those who found a way to own their own plantations and slaves came to be called

"Gens du Colours" in Haiti and equivalent names elsewhere, although their descendants as well as those of their slaves who now live in the United States became undifferentiated "African Americans." Names for nationalities, ethnicities, and languages often do not correspond with the shared set of things and patterned behavior we call cultures.

Many Cultures Intersect to Make a Person

Indeed, many cultures do not have names. The names we give to things carve out and set apart specific things from our sensory experience. The stuff of sensory experience changes, and we may choose to look at the same sensory information in multiple ways. All clinicians share a common set of understandings that come from their training in biomedicine, for example. We've only recently begun to call this a culture of biomedicine. But physicians work with a body of knowledge that distinguishes them from, say, nurse practitioners, and family practice physicians work with a body of knowledge distinct from that used by surgeons. We haven't yet highlighted the differences between these cultures with different names.

And the problem is far broader. Older people—whether physicians or plumbers or anthropologists—share a distinctive vantage point owing only to age, and older anthropologists typically share a body of knowledge that distinguishes them from junior faculty or graduate students, just as older plumbers typically share a body of knowledge that distinguishes them from apprentices. The knowledge of people the same age—sociologists, developmental psychologists, or airline pilots—may differ solely because some are men and some are women. Men and women the same age may work with a common body of knowledge merely because they grew up in poverty or experienced the privileges bestowed by wealthy parents. Puerto Ricans, irrespective of age, gender, and class, may use a common body of knowledge because they share an ethnic heritage, which may differ significantly from a body of knowledge shared by Mexicans. Fathers—whether Puerto Rican or Mexican, Eskimo or Navaho, whether physicians or nurse practitioners, whether old or young, rich or poor—may share a body of knowledge simply because they share the experience of being fathers. Academics, whether they live in China, Russia, Nigeria, Mexico, or America, share a distinctive culture irrespective of other

The Origin of Cultures

differences. So do the students at Moscow State University and the universities of Ibadan, Singapore, and Connecticut.

Thus, it's fair to say that no one possesses or participates in a single culture. Many sets of experiences go into making us who we are. For example, I am a man, husband, father, grandfather, college graduate (the first of my family), born in Memphis, Tennessee, United States, at a time that made me a member of the 1960s generation. Each label points to a body of knowledge and patterns of behavior that I share with others. I spent my early years in California's Central Valley, but within an enclave of southerners from Tennessee and Mississippi. I felt almost at home in West Africa when I went there to conduct research for my M.A. and Ph.D. degrees. Because I could look around and see people say and do the same things that I grew up with, it felt like I had come home when I conducted research in the West Indies. I was surprised by how comfortable I felt working with Russians—they acted so much like Americans—and by the discomfort I felt among Eskimo in Alaska and the Russian Far East, because they acted so differently. Similarly, I'm a fisherman, shooter, writer, and small farmer. I'm not a musician, urbanite, New Yorker, or Vietnam veteran, so what I share with people who are comes from other ways in which our life experiences intersect. In this way, I'm like you. Each of us stands at the intersection of many different cultures that we share with many other people. The specific combination of cultures that comprise that intersection sets each person apart from others. That goes a long way to making each of us different. But that also makes each of us a part of many cultures, some of which may extend around the globe.

A Thing, *Sui Generis*

The anthropologist Leslie White called culture a thing *sui generis*, meaning that it fit into no other category, that it comprised a thing unique among all that we know. Alfred Kroeber, in a similar vein, pointed out that we don't have to study individual minds to study culture because it possesses properties that go far beyond individuals, even if individuals are its only respositors. If a specialist dies, that bit of culture goes to the grave with him or her. But most of culture forms the environment into which we arrive as infants, changes independently of how we might want it to change, and requires our attention however much we may detest it. You can't wish culture away, any more than you can wish away the rising and setting of the sun and the phases of the moon. Because culture possesses qualities that go beyond the organisms that create, bear, and change it, Kroeber called culture a superorganic phenomenon.

Culture exhibits these qualities because, as John Searle observes, it consists of an agreement among people about a set of assumptions in which certain things exist and that certain things count as other things in specific contexts. Moreover, because they exist, we should do this rather than that, and we should not do something else. For example, language consists of a set of assumptions and rules that allow you to recognize significantly different sounds, assemble sounds into meaningful units, and assemble meaningful units into intelligible sentences. English distinguishes between the sounds /p/ and /b/, which make the difference between /pill/ and /bill/. In English, the sounds /s/, /z/, and /iz/ or /ez/ mean plural, but only for nouns, as in /pits/, /clocks/, /boys/, /dishes/, or /glasses/. In English, the sound /m/ may form a part of word, but by itself it doesn't mean anything—though it may signal thoughtfulness. In the West African language called Bassa, the sound /m/ may mean /you/ or /me/ depending on whether or not you say it with a low tone or a high tone. If you use one set of rules to say something and another person uses (approximately) the same set of rules to decode and understand it, you both speak the same language. If one of you uses a different set of rules, you don't. Mutual intelligibility or unintelligibility thus differentiates one language from another. Different sets of rules produce /a monyea; na fenuta/, /pazhalsta, ya magu gavaritz Dima/, and /quelle heure est-il/. We call these outcomes of different sets of rules Kru, Russian, and French, respectively.

Similarly, money consists of a set of assumptions and rules that allow you use certain things as a store of value, a measure of worth, and a means of exchange. The earliest forms of money may have been beads or shells or things that had intrinsic value like pepper, iron, pigs, or bread. Today, we recognize pieces of metal and paper with specific kinds of markings as forms of money, but in our daily living we've increasingly come to accept as money distinctive electronic transactions made with plastic cards. You may detest the concept of money, but without it you'll be hard pressed to acquire the daily necessities of food, shelter, and clothing.

The Origin of Cultures

Cultures thus make us do things, whether to speak or buy food according to its specific rules. It's simple to create your own examples from daily activities. Write down the things you do in the course of an ordinary day. For any of these things, ask yourself what would happen if you acted differently. What if you got out of bed at 5 AM or 3 PM? What would happen if you did not go to school, or did not show up at work, or did not fix the children's breakfast? If you walk to work, what would happen if you walked down the middle of the street rather than on the sidewalk? If you drive, what would happen if you drove on the left side of the road rather than the right, paid no attention to stop signs or stoplights, and parked in the middle of the street or on a sidewalk instead of a designated parking location? The answers to questions like these identify both the activities you share with others, how your activities coordinate with those of others who participate in the same culture, and the cultural norms that rationalize what you and others do and don't do. If you put in the time, you'll describe many different cultures—your family culture and other cultures that pertain to school, work, dating, and sex, to name only a few.

Culture, from one point of view, is merely an idea, an abstraction and generalization about what people think and do. A.R. Radcliffe-Brown, a prominent anthropologist in the mid-20th century, once quipped that to say that culture did things was like claiming that a quadratic equation could commit murder. Quadratic equations can't murder, but cultures can. Cultures can murder as well as do many other things because we experience this abstraction and generalization about what people think and do through the repetitive behavior of other people, as a thing. Because you encounter repetitive behavior, you create expectations, you make comparisons between what you think and do and what you know others think and do, and you anticipate consequences because the consequences matter. The foundational assumptions of cultures thus tell us to make one choice rather than another and to do one thing rather than another.

Conflicts mean clashing cultural assumptions. These may appear as conflicts between populations, perhaps as overt violence, as between jihadists who assume that Allah constitutes the highest authority for human affairs, Shari'a constitutes the ultimate law for all humans, and apostasy consists of any rejection of the first two principles and constitutes a crime punishable by death, and others who reject these assumptions. Because each of us participates in multiple cultures, these also may appear as internal conflicts. Conflicts within the set of your own cultures induce emotional trauma, as between a choice of an abortion or of carrying to term a Down syndrome child. We may do unimaginably horrific things even while conflicting cultural assumptions tear us apart, as Christopher Browning reminds us in his 1993 book *Ordinary Men*. Five hundred of such men, in only 4 months, murdered 38,000 Jews in Poland and sent another 45,000 to Treblinka because they came to a collective agreement that they should do so. Jihad by another name.

Significant cultural change thus entails a change in assumptions.

Galton's Problem

In 1889, Tylor presented a talk to the Royal Anthropological Institute which explained variations in marriage and descent practices by reference to the needs of individuals and the social effects of different practices. One member of the audience, Sir Francis Galton, pointed out that similarities between cultures might reflect either a common history or geographical closeness or both and have nothing to do with the effects of a social practice. What became known as Galton's Problem was born when Tylor couldn't rule out the common history or geographical closeness explanations.

Galton's Problem is this: Does cultural sharing come about because individuals respond to the world of experience in common ways (independent invention), or take their culture with them when they move (descent), or because individuals borrow from their neighbors (diffusion)? People do all three, of course. Shortly after the independent origins of agriculture in Southwest Asia, around 6,500 years ago, Proto Indo-Europeans, for example, emerged as a cattle-keeping population of farmers and fishers in the steppe region around the Black Sea. From there, they spread over all of Europe, much of Southwest Asia, and South Asia. They took their language with them, and it evolved into thousands of regional dialects, the descendants of which subsequently spread over the entire world to become languages spoken by more than 3,000,000,000 people. The most prominent of these languages is the one you're reading, English, which has become internationalized and used by speakers of every other language on the planet. Languages like Chinese, Grebo, and Algonkian may be related to English, but the differences are so vast that we cannot tell for sure. Languages like German, Russian, Hindi, Greek, Latin, and Persian, by contrast, share with each other and English many obvious similarities that point to descent from a single Proto Indo-European ancestor.

Robert L. Bee published the most recent summary of anthropologists' ideas about culture change in 1974. His book contained no summary about what anthropologists know about cultural dynamics. Anthropologists didn't agree, and the answers they had arrived at left too many questions unanswered. The state of the field remains largely the same. The questions first made explicit in the 19ᵗʰ century of where new cultural things come from, how they become concentrated in collective agreements and patterned behavior, and how and under what circumstances cultures either change or persist largely the same way remain central questions without a coherent answer. Galton's Problem hasn't gone away.

Evolutionary anthropologists, however, reformulated the problem as a distinction between individual learning by trial-and-error and social learning by copying. Although Tylor's original definition of culture in 1871 emphasized that it was something we learn, he never explained how, precisely, we learn it. In 1957, Noam Chomsky proposed that language learning assumed the existence of a specific neural structure. In 1962, Clifford Geertz proposed that humans had no choice but to create culture because the evolutionary processes that created us had made it a necessary product of the way human minds work. In 1969, John Bowlby argued more specifically that, among humans, mother-child attachments reflected evolved behavioral mechanisms that protected children from predators. These challenges to the Tylorian distinction between learned and nonlearned things suggested that we had evolved specific neural architectures, or modules, that regulated human behavior. By 1992, the search for these modules had come to be called evolutionary psychology. Evolutionary psychologists drew the conclusion that patterns of and for behavior emerged from a large number of built-in modes of mental processing. There's one for language learning, another for cheating detection, and others for mate selection, for different kinds of social attachments, and for all the other important domains of human activity. Jointly, these mental modules produce ecologically adaptive behavior for individuals.

Because people plainly engage in much learning from each other, this doesn't make a lot of sense. Indeed, we now know that action or the observation of action activates a specific system of neurons in the premotor cortex and inferior parietal cortex, appropriately called mirror neurons. These allow us to mirror the behavior of others in our own and may allow us to intuit the reasons why others may act one way or another. But neither does the contrary claim made by dual inheritance theorists Robert Boyd and Peter Richarson in 1985, that culture consists solely of things that are acquired and transmitted between (descent) or within (diffusion) generations, make sense. When many people are subject to equivalent experiences at roughly the same time, many "simultaneous" innovations may occur. The most prominent examples consist of the roughly simultaneous origins of agriculture in East Asia, Southeast Asia, South Asia, the Middle East, East Africa, West Africa, Mesoamerica, and South America; of metallurgy in the Middle East, the west central coast of South America, Mesoamerica, and around the Great Lakes and Northwest Coast of North America; and of civilization in the Nile River delta, Mesopotamia, the Indus River Valley, the Yellow River basin, the Valley of Mexico, and the west-central coast of South America in what is now Peru.

When people experience equivalent things at very different times, they still may arrive at the same conclusions. For example, in 1987 James Boster presented evidence from Jivaro Indians who live in the Peruvian tropical forest and college students in Kentucky consistent with the claim that human brains recognize the same patterns in sensory experience without having to learn from each other the pertinent distinctions. My own research over the last 15 years and related work by Catherine Fuentes shows, likewise, that people who have had no opportunity to interact, who grew up in places as diverse and distinct as the West Indian islands, rural eastern Connecticut, an American Indian reservation on California's north coast, and the Arctic regions of both North America and the Russian Far East, all agree that hitting and words that demean constitute violence and that hugging and words that praise constitute forms of social support and affection.

The Origin of Cultures

The Argument in This Book

This book takes the view that there's no meaningful difference between individual learning and social learning. When you think about it, it would make no sense for living things to evolve an ability to create new ideas or behavior that did not include the ability to do so with information from other things, whether living or not. A 2002 report by Simon Reader and Kevin Laland tells us, indeed, that's what happened in recent primate evolution. Human minds process information about and, so, learn from sensory fields that encompass both non-living and living things, and we learn as much from what we see other people (or other things, animate or not) not do as from what they do. And, to judge from the data presented by Etienne Danchin and his research team in 2004, studies of birds, rodents, and fish suggest that we're not alone. As I argued in 1989, our creative learning abilities may exceed those of other species by many orders of magnitude, and in some ways differ in kind, but the mental processes that generate them must have originated millions of years earlier than we previously imagined. As Roy D'Andrade pointed out in 2002, what sets us apart is language.

Whether we call it individual learning, social learning, copying, imitation, diffusion, acculturation, independent invention, or some other name, each of us learns by creating what, for us, constitutes a new idea or form of behavior and both ideas and behavior arise from the same mental process. Our minds use one mechanism to take information from the sensory fields in which we exist to create new ways to act and think about the world all the time, automatically, largely unconsciously, unexpectedly, and with error. Because no one can learn through directed teaching about institutionalized assumptions and norms by authorities without error, social learning can't take place without individual trial-and-error learning. Our minds use a second mechanism to assign emotional weights to the consequences of new things. These emotional weights distinguish bad from good and induce behavior that makes the things that produce bad effects disappear, the things that produce good effects spread, and the things that make no difference either disappear or spread or just linger, depending on random and minor influences. Selection concentrates the things that, jointly, produce still better effects.

Selected Bibliography

Barkow J.H., Cosmides, L., & Tooby, J. (Eds.) (1992). *The adapted mind: Evolutionary psychology and the generation of culture.* New York: Oxford University Press.

Bee, R.L. (1974). *Patterns and processes.* New York: Free Press.

Boster, J. (1987). Agreement between biological classification systems is not dependent on cultural transmission. *American Anthropologist, 89,* 914–920.

Bowlby, J. (1969). *Attachment and loss.* New York: Basic Books.

Boyd, R. & Richerson, P. (1985). *Culture and the evolutionary process.* Chicago: University of Chicago Press.

Browning, C.R. (1993). *Ordinary men: Reserve Battalion 101 and the Final Solution in Poland.* New York: HarperCollins.

Chomsky, N. (1957). *Syntactic structures.* The Hague: Mouton.

Danchin, E., Giraldeau, L.A., Valone, T.J., & Wagner, R.H. (2004). Public information: From nosy neighbors to cultural evolution. *Science, 305,* 487–491.

D'Andrade, R. (2002). Cultural Darwinism and language. *American Anthropologist, 104,* 223–232.

Darwish, N. (2008). *Cruel and unusual punishment.* Nashville, TN: Thomas Nelson.

Fuentes C. (2008). Pathways from interpersonal violence to sexually transmitted infections: A mixed-method study of diverse women. *Journal of Women's Health, 17,* 1591–1603.

Geertz, C. (1962). The growth of culture and the evolution of mind. In J. Sher (Ed.), *Theories of the mind* (pp. 713–740). New York: Free Press

Handwerker, W.P. (1989). The origins and evolution of culture. *American Anthropologist, 91,* 313–326.

Handwerker, W.P. (1997). Universal human rights and the problem of unbounded cultural meanings. *American Anthropologist, 99,* 799–809.

Handwerker, W.P. (1999). Cultural diversity, stress, and depression: Working women in the Americas. *Journal of Women's Health & Gender-Based Medicine, 8,* 1303–1311.

Israeli R. (2002). A manual of Islamic fundamentalist terrorism. *Terrorism and Political Violence, 14,* 23–40

Jihad Against Jews and Crusaders, World Islamic Front Statement (1998). Online at http://www.fas.org/irp/world/para/docs/980223-fatwa.htm

Kroeber, A.L. & Kluckhohn, C. (1952). *Culture: A critical review of concepts and definitions.* New York: Vintage Books.

Mansfield, L. (2006). *His own words: A translation of the writings of Dr. Ayman Al-Zawahiri.* Unspecified location: TLG Publications.

McBrearty, S. & Brooks, A. (2000). The revolution that wasn't: A new interpretation of the origin of modern human behavior. *Journal of Human Evolution, 39,* 453–563.

Noor, F.A. (2006). We should not fear being called radical—interview with Abu Bakaar Bashir. *Al Jazeera,* August, 21. Online at http://english.aljazeera.net/archive/2006/08/2008410133657429527.html.

Qutb, S. (2007 [1964]). *Milestones.* Unspecified location: Maktabah Publishers. http://web.youngmuslims.ca/online_library/books/milestones/hold/index_2.htm

Raphaeli N. (2002). Ayman Muhammad Rabi' Al-Zawahiri: The making of an arch terrorist. *Terrorism and Political Violence,* 14, 1–22

Reader, S.M. & Laland, K.N. (2002). Social intelligence, innovation, and enhanced brain size in primates. *Proceedings of the National Academy of Science,* 99, 4436–4441.

Searle, J.R. (1995). *The construction of social reality.* New York: Free Press.

Tylor, E. (1871). *Primitive culture.* New York: J.P. Putnam's Sons.

Wolf, E. (1982). *Europe and the people without history.* Los Angeles: University of California Press.

CHAPTER TWO

What Makes a Door?

In the second edition of his book *Yanomamo*, published in 1977, the anthropologist Napoleon Chagnon tells the story of a visit to Caracas, Venezuela, with his Yanomamo friend, Rerebawa. For as long as anyone remembered, the Yanomamo lived in relative isolation in the rainforests along the border of Venezuela and Brazil. That was changing rapidly with the arrival of more missionaries, mission stations, and even tourists. Chagnon became increasingly concerned that his Yanomamo friends and acquaintances needed to understand the threat posed by these changes. He tried unsuccessfully to convey a sense of the wider world of which the Yanomamo were a tiny part. Yanomamo seemed to think of the places he tried to describe, like Washington, DC, or Caracas, as just another large Yanomamo village (*shabono*). Finally, Chagnon decided that the best way to convey the threat that concerned him was to show a Yanomamo first-hand what was out there.

Rerebawa took with him some ashes to mix with his tobacco in case the people of Caracas did not cook over fires made on the floor of their houses. Although Rerebawa had seen planes land in the bush, he had never flown in one and, when he learned that he should strap himself into the seat, was concerned that the plane might crash into the upper layer of the world. When they landed outside Caracas, Rerebawa immediately recognized the large hangar as the den of the creature in which he had ridden. Chagnon asked him to get into a car to ride into the city while he collected their baggage from the plane. After Chagnon pointed out the car, Rerebawa walked around it puzzled, studied it closely, and, finally, dove through the open window.

Rerebawa did not get in the car door because he did not see a door. A door consists of two parts, one a solid thing that fills a space through which you might pass, the other a means to open the solid thing (hinges, a door handle) to allow you to do so. A Yanomamo *sha-bono* consisted of a large, round space enclosed with saplings, sometimes as much as 100 yards in diameter, with a thatched roof open above the center of a central plaza, and surrounded by a palisade of logs about 10 feet high. Yanomamo residences consisted of unclosed spaces under the *shabono*'s roof, which extended upward about 30 feet from the outside wall. Individual residences, which extend one after another around the circumference, were marked off from their neighbors only by roof supports. A Yanomamo *shabono* thus approximates a very large house that varied in size by the number of residents. Yanomamo villages and residences contained no doors. You enter a *shabono* through an opening only 3 to 5 feet high. Rerebawa thus did not see the door because he did not know what a door was because doors were completely outside his range of experience.

The things of our world of experience consist of ideas. We take for granted that a material world exists independently of our imagining. But that world doesn't tell us what's there. We have to guess at its parts and how they fit together, or how they don't. We do so by making assumptions about what's there. All human knowledge rests on assumptions. Assumptions are true by definition. They can't be proved. All assumptions probably contain errors, some are plainly wrong, but some assumptions prove useful. We label important ones and, however ambiguously in specific cases, we differentiate one from another by defining each by a set of properties. A door is a door, not a chair, a house, or a person, although there are many kinds of doors. A chair is a thing you can sit on—it has a more-or-less flat surface about 18" by 18" square placed at varying distances (ordinarily at least 6" and no more than 24") above the ground by stabilizing supports we call legs and an attached vertical surface we call a back. We call the same thing with a round surface a stool. We call the same thing without a back and with a larger surface a table.

Many people know what doors are. Many fewer realize that a woman can marry a ghost and bear his children, or that a married woman with children can marry another woman and father still more children as the husband of the new wife. Yet, ghost marriages occurred among groups as dissimilar as Nuer pastoralists in the southern Sudan and Chinese migrants to Singapore. Female

The Origin of Cultures

husbands occurred among the Fon of Dahomey and more than thirty other African societies, including the Nuer.

Our knowledge of the world consists of systems of ideas that we construct in our imaginations without being conscious of doing so. Some may strike you as quite fanciful. All consist of an identifiable set of things bound together by identifiable relations. Over the course of our lives, each of us constructs these things, and modifies them, out of the unique set and sequence of experiences that mark the trajectory of our life.

Most important, we don't control this process. We can't stop it, start it, or wish it away. As Clifford Geertz surmised, our brains process sensory information in ways that make it inevitable.

What Exists Now Shapes What Comes Next

In his 1977 collection of essays *Ever Since Darwin*, Steven Jay Gould tells the story of how 18th-century biologists engaged in a hot debate over the question of how an egg becomes a functioning organism. Epigeneticists argued that eggs were transformed into functioning organisms by a demonstrable process of embryological development. They could not, however, explain how this process originated without positing a mystical vitalism. Preformationists believed that there was nothing mystical about the process, but that to understand embryological development one had to look behind superficial appearances. They argued that the parts of functioning organisms were already in the egg. All eggs contained a perfect miniature of the adult organism, a homunculus. If this was so, embryological development merely entailed changes in the size and proportion of the parts. And if so, each egg contained another, still smaller, homunuclus; each egg in each homunculus contained another, still smaller, homunculus; ad infinitum.

Today, the idea of a homunculus may strike us as absurd. But, as Gould reminds us, in the 18th century, people believed that human history spanned only a few thousand years. Moreover, they had no cell theory to explain that organisms could not exist below a minimal size. Gould summarizes his account of these debates with this:

> Most great debates are resolved at Aristotle's golden mean, and [the debate between preformationists and epigeneticists] is no exception. From our perspective today, the epigeneticists were

right; organs differentiate sequentially from simpler rudiments during embryological development; there are no preformed parts. But the preformationists were also right in insisting that complexity cannot arise from formless raw material—that there must be something within the egg to regulate its development. All we can say (as if it mattered) is that they incorrectly identified this "something" as preformed parts, where we now understand it as encoded instructions built of DNA. But what else could we expect from eighteenth-century scientists, who knew nothing of the player piano, not to mention the computer program? The idea of a coded program was not part of their intellectual equipment. (1977:205–206)

In short, we can't imagine something new unless we start with a prototype from which we can build it. From a slightly different point of view, this means that we can't understand something new if we can't find a way to integrate it with something from our prior experience. Thus, Chagnon writes (1977:143) that Rerebawa

enjoyed himself in Caracas but was happy to return to his village, and spoke grandiloquently to his peers about the size of [the city]. "Is it bigger than Patanowa-teri's [village]?" they asked him skeptically, and he looked at me, somewhat embarrassed, and knew that he could not explain it to them. We both knew that they would not be able to conceive of what Rerebawa had seen. His arm stretched out and he described a large arc, slowly, saying with the greatest of exaggeration his language permitted: "it stretches from here to... way over... there!" And they clicked their tongues, for it was bigger than they imagined.

As Gould concluded about the difficulties that 18th-century biological scientists faced when trying to imagine that eggs contained encoded DNA (1977:206):

And, come to think of it, what could be more fantastic than the claim that an egg contains thousands of instructions, written on molecules that tell the cell to turn on and off the production of certain substances that regulate the speed of chemical processes? The notion of preformed parts sounds far less contrived to me. The only thing going for coded instructions is that they seem to be there.

Biological scientists in the mid-20th century faced an equivalent dilemma and dismissed as fantasy (or, bad science) Barbara McClintock's discovery that genes and other genetic elements can move around the genome. In 1866, Gregor Mendel showed that inheritance did not blend features of the parents, which contradicted the prevailing view at the time and one that continued to dominate the assumptions of biologists for another 30 years. The assumption that inheritance involved blending disappeared in the first years of the 20th century after the discovery of chromosomes as the bearers of Mendel's units of inheritance. By 1909, we called these things genes, recognized that they came in pairs (called alleles), and came to think of them as fixed, discrete points on pairs of chromosomes. McClintock's "findings" thus made no sense. She had to be wrong. The identification of the molecular construction of DNA by James Watson and Francis Crick in 1953 made possible the development of molecular biology after 1960, which subsequently revealed that parts of a gene might be located on different chromosome pairs, that most of the material that made up chromosomes did not constitute genes, and that, indeed, genes do jump around. McClintock won the Nobel Prize in 1983.

New Things Come from Old Things

Despite the thingness qualities culture exhibits as a collective agreement, only individuals learn and individuals constitute the only respositors of cultural knowledge. In his 1932 book *Remembering*, F.C. Bartlett made the observation that each of us constructs our understanding of the world by combining things we perceive with things we remember. In his 1953 book *Innovation*, Homer Barnett added the observation that this constructive process necessarily created new things, qualitatively different from other things, and he exhaustively reviewed the ways in which new things came into being.

Barnett argued that we construct new things by a simple process. If by assumption we make one thing (or a part of one thing) the same as another thing (or, one or more of its parts), each counts as the same thing and one may substitute for the other. New things come into being when we substitute one thing for another. The result is something qualitatively different from the old things from which they are made. The new thing may consist of a new idea. Albert Einstein, for example, knew from Galileo via Newton that a fixed frame for evaluating the movement of one object relative to another did not exist, and that the laws of physics applied to all frames of reference.

Traveling home after many hours discussing a conflict between Newtonian and Maxwellian physics with his friend Michele Besso, Einstein imagined that if you looked at a clock while moving away from it at the speed of light that the clock would appear to be stopped, while the clock in your hand would indicate the passage of time normally. This meant that it was impossible to define time independent of a frame of reference and that what counts as a unit of time depended on velocity. He thus recognized that objects which move at the same speed as each other (an inertial frame) counted as one among many frames of reference. He substituted this specific kind of frame for the set of all frames and concluded that the laws of physics are the same in all inertial frames. He knew from Maxwell that the speed of light, c, was a constant. If the speed of light is a constant, it must count as a law of physics, so the speed of light must be a constant in all inertial frames. He thus created his two principles of Special Relativity. The world hasn't been the same since.

Einstein also knew from Leibniz that energy (E) equals the mass of an object (m) times the square of its velocity (v) and from Lorentz that mass (m) grows as its velocity approaches the speed of light (c). Einstein recognized that, if mass grows with velocity, the energy in velocity must count as a form of mass and mass must count as a form of energy. Simple calculations show that $E=mc^2$, which tells us that even small stones may release huge amounts of energy. The mental processes by which Einstein transformed our world are no different in kind than the ones that Rerebawa plausibly employed to recognize that a door counts as a kind of blockage and manipulation of a door handle counts as a kind of blockage removal, which makes opening a door the same as moving aside branches that block a forest trail.

The new thing may consist of an object. Player pianos came into being after someone equated holes in a paper roll with fingers that could strike a piano key and recognized that a specific pattern of holes would code for the specific pattern of key strokes that produced a musical score. Edwin Votey made the first useful player piano in 1895. But the idea of coded holes in paper goes back to 1725 and provided the basis for constructing a loom for weaving intricate patterns.

The Origin of Cultures

Herman Hollerith borrowed this idea from his brother-in-law, who was in the silk-weaving business and who had told him about the looms for Jacquard weaving, to produce cards with which to process the 1890 U.S. census. Hollerith cards were, in retrospect, a critical step in the development of information technologies.

As Barnett pointed out, we substituted horses for people to turn millstones, presses, waterlifts, and treadmills. Later, we substituted engines for horses in these and other activities to create the material basis of the Industrial Revolution. Active development of engines followed from Torricelli's announcement in 1643 that air exerts pressure at sea level. Soon afterward, people tried to use this pressure to do things by creating a vacuum into which air would force a piston. In 1654, van Guericke constructed a pump that drew air instead of water from a closed container. In 1680, Huygens substituted gunpowder for a pump. Huygen's assistant, Denis Papin, substituted steam for gunpowder when he reasoned that water vapor had a force like air. Papin constructed an engine and demonstrated its ability to raise a counterweight in the presence of the members of the Royal Society of London. In the early 1700s, Thomas Newcomen constructed a heavy-duty replica of Papin's laboratory exhibit that pumped water from mines instead of raising blocks, and replaced horses on treadmills. In 1769, James Watt placed the condenser in its own chamber to transform Newcomen's design into a much more efficient and useful steam engine. Huygens's experiments with gunpowder as a source of controlled force also took another direction. In the 1780s, Alessandro Volta showed that an electrical spark could explode air (mixed with hydrogen) and, in 1799, LeBon built a machine powered by exploding coal gas. In 1859, Lenoir substituted benzene for gas, substituted his piston and combustion chamber for the comparable elements of a steam engine, and mounted his engine on a carriage or a wagon as a substitute for horse or steam power. He thus produced the first useful vehicle driven by an internal combustion engine.

What Exists Now Could Not Exist Without What Went Before

Because new things arise as new combinations of old things, cultural change exhibits the properties of evolutionary change. This means that what exists now could not exist without what went before. This means, too, that the things of the moment set the options for our immediate future. Judaism, for example, arose among some farmers and pastoralists of the Middle East around 4,000 years ago. The development of Jewish theology later gave rise to two of the other great world religions, Christianity and Islam.

Jewish theology holds that, 4,000 years ago, God chose the collective descendants of Abraham as his people, promised them protection and a special place in the world, and set in motion the development of Judaism. By 2,500 years ago, Jews thought of their god as the one and only ruler of the universe, who rewarded good and punished evil. Ritual practices were important, but community ethics that emphasized fairness, justice, and doing good were even more so. Evil, they believed, existed independently, although it could make individuals do evil things. At the end of time, however, a messiah ("anointed one") who embodied both religious and political-military leadership qualities would defeat the forces of evil and produce justice in the after-life.

These conclusions came after much winnowing. A thousand years earlier, it was still permissible to acknowledge and worship other gods. The idea of the end of time and an afterlife did not exist. The Jewish god might do evil if his chosen people did not obey him properly. The set of laws delivered by Moses provided the foundation for a Jewish nation, but the emphasis on ritual practices was easily corrupted as the Israelites settled in Canaan and created an increasingly complex, stratified, and secular society with Saul as its first king. His successor, King David, made Jerusalem its capital, united the tribes of Israel into a single kingdom, and established an empire that ruled over defeated neighboring states. A standing army, heavy taxes, and forced labor came with the new absolute monarchy. These grew worse under the third monarch, Solomon, who built a magnificent palace and an enormous temple, and paid for it in land and slave labor. These events made clear that individuals, with no help from God, could do evil themselves. The prophets built on this observation to suggest that God might be the source of justice. This emphasized the importance of good done by individuals and gave community ethics a new importance.

After Solomon's death, around 3,000 years ago, the northern tribes revolted and the Hebrew empire that David created fell apart to become two smaller and weaker kingdoms: Israel in the north with its capital Samaria, and Judaea in the south with its capital

The Origin of Cultures

Jerusalem. These fell prey to their more powerful neighbors in Egypt and Mesopotamia who coveted the important trade routes through Jewish territory. The Assyrians conquered Israel about 2,700 years ago, dispersed the ten northern tribes throughout their territory, who disappeared from Jewish history. Rule over Mesopotamia shifted from Assyrians to Babylonians. Judeans, caught between Egyptian and Babylonian rivals, shifted loyalties once too often. Although their god had promised protection and a special place in the world, shifting politics in the Middle East and bad decisions by Judaean leaders resulted, about 2,600 years ago, in exile to Babylon of the Jewish elite, the burning of Jerusalem, and the destruction of Solomon's Temple by Nebuchadnezzar.

Cyrus conquered Babylonia about 50 years later in the process of creating a Persian empire and sent the exiles home to rebuild Jerusalem, erect a second Temple, and return to the worship of their god. The returning Jews brought with them an explanation for the devastation they had suffered—evil existed, quite independently of humans. This they borrowed from the Persian religion, Zoroastrianism. The premise that evil constituted a thing in and of itself stimulated theorizing about the end of time, an afterlife, and a messiah, anointed, like Jewish priests and kings, who would overcome evil to create a just world in the afterlife.

By 2,060 years ago, Judaea came under Roman rule. Judaea in Roman times, like in earlier Jewish empire times, was characterized by a sharply stratified population. An elite set of administrators, priests, and absentee landlords aligned with Rome. Artisans, servants, slaves, and small farmers and herders who worked heavily taxed land weren't so pleased. Insurrections against social and economic injustice headed by messianic leaders began soon after the establishment of Roman rule and did not end until more than 100 years later with the capture of Masada in 73 AD. Jesus of Nazareth was one among nearly a dozen such leaders.

Christianity as we know it today rests on the premise that Jesus died to save all people from the evil that afflicts us, not just Jews. Those who acknowledge Jesus as savior enjoy an afterlife of peace and justice. Although they are expected to bring Jesus into their lives and act with compassion, goodness, and justice, they may succumb to evil. This emphasis on faith comes from Paul in his proselytizing among both

Jewish and Gentile communities outside of Judaea, well after Jesus died. A core group of early Jewish Christians led by James remained in Jerusalem, continued to worship in the temple, and maintained itself as a military-messianic cult until James died. The defeat of the Jews at Masada and the later destruction of the Temple in Jerusalem initiated the Jewish Diaspora. Having witnessed Rome crush Jewish resistance, the Jewish-Christian and Gentile-Christian communities outside of the region the Romans now called Palestine found that Paul's message posed little threat to Roman authorities. Indeed, within 150 years, they emerged as a highly successful international organization that Roman leadership co-opted by legalizing Christian worship.

Christianity thus emerged around 2,000 years ago as a failed messianic-military insurrection against Roman occupation, as Marvin Harris reminded us. By contrast, as John Wansbrough suggested, Islam emerged about 600 years later as a successful messianic-military movement. By the time of Muhammad, communities of Jews and Jewish-Christians were found throughout the polytheistic Middle East. From these, Muhammad borrowed the idea of a single, all powerful god whom followers should obey, a written text, a chosen people (Muhammad identified Arabs as descendants of Abraham through his son Ishmael), a holy city (initially Jerusalem but later Mecca), a messianic prophet (himself), resurrection, heaven and hell, and the devil. Like the Jewish messianic prophets of Judaea in Roman times who responded to the inequities of Roman rule and the Jewish elite, Muhammad came from a relatively poor family and attracted as followers others significantly dissatisfied with the inequities that characterized Meccan society.

The success of Christianity owed much to a message that offered salvation to individuals while not threatening political authority. The success of Islam owed much to not having to face Roman legions, or Persian troops, at their strongest. Both empires had begun to crumble. Roman expansion began about the time Jews returned from exile in Babylonia and attained its greatest size about 1,900 years ago. Within 200 years, the empire began to split between East and West, and the Western empire collapsed entirely 200 years later when Alaric sacked Rome. Although the Eastern empire (Byzantium) continued for another 1,000 years when Constantinople (now, Istanbul) fell to the

Ottoman Turks in 1453, its early history was marked on its western borders by constant assault from Germanic tribes. In the east, fighting between the Byzantine and Persian empires weakened both and created opportunities for newly emerging competitors.

The success of Islam also owed much to three innovations by Muhammad. First, he added to the borrowed Judeo-Christian theology an injunction that rejection or renunciation of Islam warranted death. Second, he codified the struggle of good against evil in the concept of jihad, which could take various forms, from an inner struggle against the temptations of evil to a holy war against nonbelievers. Third, he made death in a holy war an instant path to salvation with extravagant rewards in Paradise and he gave the spoils of war to those who did not die. This combination of powerful incentives and weakened militaries made it possible for Muhammad and his religious descendants to quickly take control of both the rich east-west trade between China and Europe and the south-north trade between Africa and Europe.

Because cultures evolve, however, they make moving targets. Early Christianity evolved into Western Catholicism and Eastern Orthodoxy; Western Catholicism evolved into Roman Catholics, Anglicans, and many Protestant sects. Roman Catholicism evolved significantly different cultures in the United States, Ireland, and St. Lucia, to cite only three examples. The Protestant sects evolved into a dozens of varieties, from Methodism to Pentacostalism to Mormonism. Early Islam evolved into Sunnis and Shi'as. Mystics from both created Sufism. Salafism (or Wahhabism) evolved out of Sunni beliefs, and the current jihad-by-the-sword, which killed both Ayat and Rachel, evolved out of elements of both Sunni and Shi'a doctrine, the innovations Muhammad added to Judeo-Christian thought to make it distinctively Islamic.

Why Cultures *Must* Evolve, *Unexpectedly*

In 1989, I suggested that brains can construct new things if and only if the genes that construct the brain and the senses that feed it information do not dictate the content of the ideas our minds produce. The neural circuitry that makes this possible necessarily creates a new level of things that we call ideas, constructs, models, schemas, or theories. It also makes this emergent property of our minds, construct formation, an inferential process. We *must* guess at the things that make up the world and how they're organized. We guess based on prior knowledge, which consists of constructs that we created in our minds on the basis of our unique and limited past experiences. Because we have to make guesses about the things that comprise our world of experience, we can create things like ghost marriages and female husbands and chairs and tables and people. We can't help it. Our minds do this for us without our direction.

The processes by which we construct our understanding of the world integrate sensory information with information from various forms of memory and, necessarily, create new things. Because the process means, at the level of consciousness, making guesses, we can't help but make mistakes. We search for an hour for glasses that we've been wearing all along. We overrate our abilities or underrate them. We write an equation incorrectly, as was one of the equations in Einstein's 1905 paper that introduced the world to Special Relativity. We misjudge people and find ourselves betrayed. The most notoriously unreliable evidence consists of eyewitness testimony. We can't see clearly, so we argue over whether or not the world's climate is undergoing a gradual warming. If we agree with the idea of global warming, we argue about why it began and what to do about it. Some people believe that the world is engaged in a war between radical fundamentalist Islam in the form of jihadists and civilization as we know it. Others don't. Larry Johnston, a former assistant director at the U.S. Department of State's Office of Counterterrorism argued persuasively in an op-ed in the *New York Times* on July 10, 2001, that the threat of terrorism was grossly overblown. Because each of us can draw only on our own limited prior experience, we don't see the world perfectly; we rely heavily on others to find our errors. But even when we have excellent advice and all the information necessary to see clearly, we make silly decisions, as Barbara Tuchman documented in her 1987 book *The March of Folly* beginning with the prototype decision by the Trojans to accept a gift horse filled with Greek warriors. In fact, the more a living thing relies on this form of information processing, the more mistakes it makes.

I called this process intelligence. Intelligent beings think in ways that invariably lead to new and unexpected ways of looking at the world. They thus generate an unusual degree of behavioral flexibility.

The Origin of Cultures

All living things, plants as well as people, must process information from sensory fields. That processing may or may not involve information storage or the integration of stored information with information recently received. But to say that an intelligent mind creates ideas does not mean that genes cease to influence behavior in important ways. Ideas are coded bundles of information that are more than the sum of their parts because they integrate information from a variety of senses, including information about the relationship among ideas. Specific behaviors or complex sets of coordinated activities and movements embody those codes. Thus, ideas and behaviors cannot be created unless genes construct neural circuitry that allows different kinds of information from one sense to be related to different kinds of information from several or from all senses, including relationships among different forms of information. Moreover, genes dictate that experience will be stored in a particular form as one or another, or several kinds of memory, and that we will construct ideas and behavior by a process that integrates information from a variety of sources within specific constraints of time and complexity. Genes thus control the processes by which intelligent minds work. They just don't dictate the outcome. Intelligent forms of life thus have a built-in mechanism that continuously generates random conceptual innovation and behavioral change (see Box 2.1).

Random (maybe chaotic) processes intrude on the constructive process of information transmission within and between cell assemblies, however. Neural processing is ephemeral and may become blocked by weak synaptic links; traces may linger that may facilitate the re-creation of a specific firing pattern, or of any part of one; and different cell assemblies may overlap or otherwise intrude on each other. In the process, they may drop features, add them, or substitute one thing for another. Our brains thus invariably and necessarily produce the variation we see in our ideas and behavior. No two experiences come to us the same way, and no experience of the same thing duplicates earlier ones. This means that each of us cannot help but see the world differently at different times and places, act in ways that may surprise us, and make mistakes. The manner in which they produce ideas necessarily involve substitutions of the kind that produce new things.

BOX 2.1. Thinking a Thought, Making New Things

In 1996, William Calvin suggested a means by which the brain actually accomplishes this. In the late 1940s, the psychologist Donald Hebb observed that associative memory seemed to stem from groups of neurons that work together when processing sensory input. Neurons consist of dendrites that receive information from the axons of other neurons across a synapse. Information passes through neurons as electrical impulses. Information passes across a synapse in the form of a chemical (a neurotransmitter, or modulator) released from an axon and taken up by a dendrite. Our neocortex, the sheath of neurons most recently added in the brain's evolution, consists largely of pyramidal neurons that run through a number of strata. The bottom two strata contain pyramidal neurons that send axons to the thalamus. The one immediately above these receives inputs from the thalamus. The top strata contain neurons with axons that branch sideways up to 10,000 times, which terminate at varying distances. The synapses of these cells tend to be characterized by distinctive circuit properties. One consists of a propensity to retain traces of earlier activity, which makes reactivation easier (long-term potentiation). The other consists of the common presence of postsynaptic receptors that strengthen the signal of inputs that arrive in clusters. Because they do not leave these strata, they thus appear to process information solely within the neocortex.

Calvin argues that the distinctive features of our neocortex provide the means for effective Hebbian cell assembly activity. Any one Hebbian cell assembly consists, minimally, of 100 minicolumns

What Sets Us Apart?

We can't precisely identify the properties we perceive and store as memory and subsequently assemble into ideas and actions. But we can identify many of the things that they allow us to discriminate among, including intentions or goals, means, and behavior, self and other, subject and object, who did what to whom, where, and why; the things that comprise sensory fields; and the sequences of facts that constitute events or episodes. This list comes from Homer Barnett, Michael Tomasello, Laureano Castro and Miguel Toro, and

The Origin of Cultures

containing around 10,000 pyramidal neurons organized in a hexagonal pattern. But cell assemblies do not consist of discrete sets of cells. Rather, they appear as mosaics of electrical activity that dynamically form and re-form across the billions and billions of neurons that make up the human neocortex. They thus create distinctive firing patterns with both spatial and temporal dimensions. The memories you accumulate from the sensory fields of your past and present consist of bits and pieces of information. Your mind doesn't remember coherent thoughts or actions. Your mind absorbs and stores things like variations in color, intensity of light, physical size and shape, odor, taste, feel, and sound as well as relationships between things, the properties of things, and events and sequences of events. Your mind constructs coherent thoughts and actions by assigning relationships to and among the bits and pieces of information of your mind. Some memories may reside in specific cells. The vast majority, more likely, consist of firing patterns that code for a piece of sensory information. To dunk a basketball or think of God, the things of our mind must undergo an assembly process of the kind Donald Hebb imagined. At any moment in time, huge numbers of cell assemblies may be active. Their activities may mutually excite each other, capture the information processes of other assemblies, and produce firing synchrony. The cell assembly, Calvin argues, may record the features of a thing and its firing patterns may code for the thing and constitute the neural analog of an idea. The entrainment process that generates synchrony determines the construction outcome.

Roy D'Andrade, and shouldn't be taken as complete. Discriminations of this kind, however, make it possible for you to recognize the intentions of living things, their mistakes and your own, and substitute yourself empathically for others and so learn from what they do or do not do. They also make it possible for you to substitute yourself for objects and imagine that a rock contains power. You may recognize the integration of that idea with others into a coherent theory. Depending on when and where you live your life, you may call that theory witchcraft or Special Relativity.

As I indicated in Chapter 1, we share many of these features of mind with creatures as diverse as birds and rodents, so the evolutionary history of this mechanism must be very, very old. Data presented in Harry Jerison's 1973 book *Evolution of the Brain and Intelligence* suggest that a mind that processed information in creative ways may have first appeared 50 million years ago and perhaps as early as 200 million years ago. Roy D'Andrade points out that the intelligence of contemporary humans owes much to the emergence of the means of effectively communicating all of this, which we call language. An ancestor who could talk about what he or she did, when, how, and why, could more readily share his or her knowledge. Sharing knowledge quickens the spread of important innovations and means that your ideas can build on those of others, even if those ideas or ways of doing things originated hundreds or thousands or hundreds of thousands of years earlier. The minds of people who store more information generate both more and more radically different new ways of thinking about the world and acting in it. This heightens personal awareness that things don't work right and makes finding ways to effectively correct mistakes easier and faster. Significant advantages thus accrued to our ancestors, who, generation after generation, possessed minds that both received and stored increasing amounts of sensory information, processed it in ways that generated increasing numbers of innovations, and effectively shared them increasingly well.

But the evolution of a mind that receives and stores several orders of magnitude more information than other living creatures, and that produces significant innovations in large quantities and quickly, doesn't make mistakes go away. The mental mechanism that assembles stored information in ways that yield lots of new things appears not to have changed much, if at all, for millions and millions of years. New things come into being unpredictably. We know that we will create new things and that the new things that emerge will come out of old things. But we can't predict what new things will appear or when. Our minds thus give us a poor ability to see the present clearly, filled as it is with errors great and small. However much we wish it otherwise, they give us an ability to see into the future even more poorly.

Selected Bibliography

Bartlett, F.C. (1932). *Remembering.* Cambridge: Cambridge University Press.

Barnett, H.G. (1953). *Innovation: The basis of cultural change.* New York: McGraw-Hill.

Barnett, H.G. (1965). Laws of socio-cultural change. *International Journal of Comparative Sociology,* 6, 207–230.

Calvin, W.H. (1996). *The cerebral code: Thinking a thought in the mosaics of the mind.* Cambridge, MA: MIT Press.

Castro, L. & Toro, M. (2004). The evolution of culture: From primate social learning to human culture. *Proceedings of the National Academy of Sciences,* 101, 10235–10240.

Chagnon, N.A. (1977). *Yanomamo: The fierce people.* New York: Holt, Rinehart & Winston.

D'Andrade, R. (2002). Cultural Darwinism and language. *American Anthropologist,* 104, 223–232.

Gould, S.J. (1977). *Ever since Darwin: Reflections in natural health.* New York: W.W. Norton & Company.

Handwerker, W.P. (1989). The origins and evolution of culture. *American Anthropologist,* 91, 313–326.

Harris, M. (1974). *Cows, pigs, wars, and witches.* New York: Random House.

Jerison, H.J. (1973). *Evolution of the brain and intelligence.* New York: Academic Press.

Mendel, G. (1950 [1866]). *Experiments on plant hybridization.* Cambridge, MA: Harvard University Press.

Tomasello, M. (1999). *The cultural origins of human cognition.* Cambridge, MA: Harvard University Press.

Tuchman, B. (1987). *The march of folly.* New York: Random House.

Wansbrough, J. (1977). *Quranic studies: Sources and methods of scriptural interpretation.* Oxford: Oxford University Press.

CHAPTER THREE

Sensory Fields
and Cultural Outputs

Normal human thinking processes generate an unceasing stream of unexpected, new ideas and new ways of doing things. We construct new ways to think and act by a process we call "inference." Thus, new ways to think about ourselves and the world we live in constitute guesses about the best way to go about living. Because no two people follow the same path through life, the material of our experience varies individually. Each of us cannot help but be different—indeed, unique—from others. You speak English, like 1.5 billion other people in today's world. But you speak English with a distinctive dialect that you acquired by virtue of your association with other language speakers, perhaps in Boston, or Singapore, or London. Because the operation of your mind produces new things all the time, incremental change occurs constantly, despite your lack of awareness. Thus, you speak this dialect in unique ways, which linguists call your idiolect. Moreover, it changes over your life time. Significant changes become codified as named things retrospectively.

Different Experiences Produce Different Cultures

The sensory fields from which our minds acquire information vary with when we arrive in the world, where our birth takes place, and the people with whom we interact, in which ways, and at what age. People exposed to different sensory fields necessarily evolve different ways of thinking about the world and acting in it. Because people everywhere respond to the world of experience in equivalent ways, people with equivalent forms of sensory experience form equivalent prototypes and discover the same things, despite never having been in contact. Shared prior experience thus may lead many people to arrive at the same conclusion independently.

For example, ongoing research with Danielle Wozniak in the Women's Sexuality Over the Life Course project has revealed that some women who learn that they have chlamydia or herpes, which people assign to the same category as sexually transmitted diseases (STDs) of reproductive organs, experience embarrassment, self-loathing, and guilt, and characteristically receive blame, discomfort, and embarrassment from others who learn of their disease. Other women who learn that they have those conditions, however, experience irritation rather than embarrassment and feel no guilt.

We do not find differences like these with diseases like cancer, heart disease, pneumonia, or flu. People who learn that they have heart disease or cancer, which belong to a category of major causes of death with genetic and life-style components, usually experience fear, feel little or no guilt for having gotten the disease, and receive much sympathy from others. People who learn that they have flu or pneumonia, which belong to a category of infectious agent–induced minor causes of death, usually experience far more irritation than fear, feel no guilt for having gotten the disease, and receive a small amount of sympathy from others. The features that differentiate STDs from diseases like these stem from variation in what women take as fundamental truths about relationships, adults, privacy, and sex. Consequently, these differences appear in the collectively agreed on and intersubjectively shared "shoulds" that we call cultural norms and that women use to reason about behavior and events that intersect these institutions. The following analysis thus focuses solely on cultural variation among women.

Women value relationships, for example, which is to say that they experience them as good things. They take for granted that life is a good thing, too, that threats to life and either emotional or physical hurts are bad things, and that feelings of joy, happiness, calm, and safety are good things. Humans are not perfect, so the individuals involved in a relationship do both good things and bad things to each other. But because hurts are bad things, involved individuals, who can be either male or female, should treat each other in ways that promote good feelings like happiness and safety. Things that count as showing respect and otherwise taking care of the other's material and emotional welfare evoke good feelings. Involved individuals thus should show each other respect and otherwise take care of each other. Women judge a partner whose patterned behavior consists primarily of things that count as showing respect and taking care of them as good, and as someone in whom they can safely place their trust. Women evaluate physicians whose patterned behavior consists primarily of things that count as showing respect and taking care of them as good doctors who provide good medical care and in whom they can safely place their trust.

Women also value adults. All communities define adults by reference to some age criterion. But chronological age takes second place to a more fundamental criterion. Adults are people who exhibit responsible, mature behavior. Things that count as such behavior include taking care of oneself and treating others with respect and care for their emotional and material welfare. Thus, adults should take care of themselves. They should also treat others with respect and care for the other's emotional and material welfare. Chronologically young people may act like adults, and are so judged when their behavior closely matches the norms for adult behavior. Chronologically old people may act like children and are so judged when their behavior badly matches the norms for adult behavior. One thing that counts as treating others with respect and care for others' emotional and material welfare is placing trust in them. A relationship with another adult thus implies the mutual expectation of trust. Indeed, engaging in such a relationship counts as a distinguishing feature of adulthood.

Women also value privacy. The label privacy applies to a domain of things that, if exposed to the view of others, may threaten things that a person values. Things that count as private include many kinds of sexual activities and an individual's genitals. Thus, one should take great care when exposing certain kinds of sexual activities or one's genitals, for to do so would cause embarrassment or worse. Because women generally value children very highly, damage to one's ability to reproduce usually counts as among the worst possible consequences.

Women also value sex, and unmarried women in their 20s and unmarried women older than 40 engage in patterns of sex that differ only superficially. Young women often practice "hook-ups"—casual, one-night relationships in which partners exchange oral sex. They also engage in intercourse with men selected because they might add to women's sexual experience and prowess, or can help women rid themselves of the liability of virginity, not because they might make a good long-term partner. Older women feel less compulsion for experimentation and tend to select partners for compatibility. But both sets of women, if unmarried, characteristically practice serial monogamy and, married or not, engage in unprotected sex.

These women take the view that, as responsible adults, they should take care of themselves, and "being careful" appeared as a theme throughout our interviews. Things that counted as being careful included not sleeping around, not having one-night stands, and not having multiple sex partners at once. For young women, hookups, which some women practice by the hundreds over any given year, do not count as sleeping around or having one-night stands because they involve oral sex and, thus, do not count as (real) sexual activity. For women of all ages, using condoms also counts as being careful. But a responsible, adult partner should not give a girl friend or wife an STD. Moreover, women should place trust in their partnerships with someone who exhibits adult behavior. One way to take care of oneself is to ask a partner about his sexual history. Partners who do not talk about a history of many sexual partners exhibit responsible, adult behavior. One way to show your trust of a responsible, adult partner is not to ask for an STD test. An older woman might use the "three date rule" and avoid intercourse until after the third date, whereas a younger woman might have intercourse on the first date with a male with whom she had developed a "deep connection," perhaps an agreement for monogamy. But women of all ages consistently apply norms for relationships and adults to sexual behavior and, consequently, expose themselves to STDs. One woman stated, "I use condoms until, well, until I don't." Only one woman reported that she asks her partners to be tested for STDs. Nonetheless, these women act in ways that count as "being careful" and thus act like responsible adults.

Women who do not protect themselves from STDs by taking these steps fail to act like a responsible adult. Hence, only irresponsible women who have lots of anonymous sex—"not taking care of yourself and having sex with lots and lots of dirty people," as one woman put it—get sexual diseases. Some women extend this conclusion, that women who get STDs have only themselves to blame, to calling "promiscuity" a female health issue.

The Origin of Cultures

Learning that one has an STD thus contradicts fundamental truths about relationships, adults, and sex, and poses significant privacy threats. The existence of an STD reveals to a woman that she deceived herself about her partner's ability to act like a responsible adult by focusing on only a small subset of behaviors. Thus, she, too, failed to act as a responsible adult. If it is possible to cure the disease, she must expose herself at least minimally to members of the health care system. The disease may threaten her reproductive potential. It also threatens her relationship potential by reducing her mate choices. She will lose some mate choices through reputation damage that follows from public knowledge of her STD. She will lose others when desirable mates break off future relationships after learning about her STD history. A woman who learns that she has chlamydia or herpes thus experiences embarrassment, self-loathing, and guilt, and receives blame, discomfort, and embarrassment from others like themselves who learn of their disease. Such women rarely confide STD histories to close friends.

The women who experience irritation rather than embarrassment when they learn they have an STD, and feel no guilt, operate with a different set of fundamental truths—that men are rutting beasts who cannot act as responsible adults and, thus, should never be trusted. A responsible adult takes care of herself. Granting a man respect, and acting in ways that place a man's emotional and material welfare on a par to one's own emotional and material welfare, thus counts as irresponsible adult behavior. Men treat STDs as a sign of their virility, so STD histories pose little threat to one's reproductive potential by lost mate choice—women with STDs are commonplace. The mere exposure of sexual activities or genitals poses no threat, so do not count as private phenomena. Because one can count on men to act irresponsibly, as a responsible adult, one cannot take responsibility for the consequences of male behavior. Consequently, if a partner infects you with an STD, you have nothing to feel embarrassment or guilt about. Like flu or cancer, STDs just happen.

Individuals derive their assumptions and the norms that follow from those assumptions from their accumulated experiences. The fundamental truths collectively agreed on and intersubjectively shared among the first set of women, for example, imply much experience

Sensory Fields and Cultural Outputs 59

with affectionate and supportive cultural environments. The fundamental truths collectively agreed on and intersubjectively shared among the second set of women imply much experience with violent and traumatic cultural environments. Catherine Fuentes's 2008 article "Pathways from Interpersonal Violence to Sexually Transmitted Infections" shows, indeed, that the qualitatively different cultural models used by these two groups of women correspond with qualitative differences in childhood histories of violence or affection and in subsequent STD histories, ability to negotiate condom use, drug/alcohol abuse, number of lifetime sexual partners, and adolescent childbearing.

Sensory Field Isolation and Information Flow

Because the material of our experience consists largely of information about the behavior of the people with whom we come into contact, cultural variation corresponds closely to the frequency and intensity of social interaction. Ordinarily, for example, we learn much from our parents and less from our grandparents or uncles and aunts. Significant changes in historical events coupled with significant interaction with peers, however, combines to create generational differences, as between grandparents who grew up with the depression and fought in World War II; parents who grew up in the prosperous years of the second half of the 20th century, the Civil Rights movement, the Vietnam War, and the sexual revolution; and children (now, parents too) who grew up with the collapse of the Soviet Union, video games, computers, and the Internet.

The frequency and intensity of social interaction varies with distance in time, space, or behavior. If you have ever spent much time alone, you probably learned that your isolation produced changes that left you with a sense of disconnectedness with your friends and family once you started to interact with them again. That's because each of us changes all the time, even if only a little. Because new cultural things come into being all the time to create differences in the sensory fields of the people we live with, cultural differences grow over time in the presence of barriers of distance, time, or behavior. Within the last 1,500 years, the breakup of the western Roman Empire produced relative isolation among Vulgar Latin–speaking populations and the subsequent evolution out of Latin of languages that we know today as Italian, Spanish, Catalan, Portuguese, French, and Romanian (and, still not widely known, Calabrese and Occitan). The Proto-German spoken perhaps 2,500 years ago evolved into Proto-Norse, South Germanic, and Anglo-Frisian. Proto-Norse evolved into Danish, Swedish, Norwegian, and Icelandic. South Germanic evolved into German, Dutch, and English. Anglo-Frisian evolved into Frisian, Scots, and English, the latter two having evolved out of Old English. The Middle English spoken around the time of William the Conqueror evolved into modern English by around 300 years ago. Modern English has since evolved many dialects—English, American, Australian, Malaysian, and West Indian, among others, each of which exhibits its own evolved dialects, like the differences between cockney and the Queen's English in the British Isles, and the English spoken in Boston and New Orleans.

By contrast, participation in a common sensory field lets you keep pace with the changes in others, even if you don't interact for long periods of time. The mutual unintelligibility by which we identify language differences, for example, did not evolve among neighboring people who maintained close ties. Swedes in the south of Sweden speak more easily to Danes across the border than they can to Swedes in the north. In West Africa, people who live in Cape Palmas and people who live 100 kilometers up the coast in Sasstown speak in ways that the other cannot understand. The people in Cape Palmas speak Grebo; the people in Sasstown speak Kru. People who live inland from Sasstown speak Kru. People who live inland from Cape Palmas speak Grebo. But Grebo spoken inland is mutually intelligible with Kru spoken inland. Inland, Grebo and Kru constitute different names for the same language. People who live in neighboring villages from Portugal to Italy through Spain, France, and Belgium speak mutually intelligible languages. As distance grows, the sensory fields that contribute to new cultural things become increasingly different, and language intelligibility shrinks. We call incremental language differences like these dialect chains.

Dialect chains, however, are just a special case of incremental cultural differences called cultural clines, which distinguish world culture regions. Thus, internal similarities and external differences distinguish

Africa (south of the Sahara) from Europe, East Asia, Southeast Asia, South Asia, the Middle East (Southwest Asia and North Africa), North America, Mesoamerica, South America, Oceania, Australia, and the Arctic. Each great culture region exhibits clinal change from one to the other. And each exhibits subregional culture areas. In Africa, for example, the peoples in the East African cattle region show marked differences from the people of the Kalahari. Within North America, the natives of the Arctic, Pacific Northwest Coast, and the Great Plains show great internal similarities and sharp external differences. In each case, however, adjacent subregions change from one to another only incrementally.

We Take Our Cultures with Us

Americans overseas create little American communities that re-create, to the extent possible, the world from which they came. These include swimming pools and swimming lessons, tennis courts and tennis lessons, and American schools built so that, inside, you can't tell if you're in Moline, Illinois, or Redding, California, or Accra, Ghana. The cultural patterns that our Foreign Service officers bring with them come predominantly from white, upper- to upper-middle class, Anglo-Saxon, Protestant America. The Chinatowns in all large cities and many smaller ones show that American WASPS aren't the only ones who do this. Indeed, many U.S. cities are famous for immigrant communities—Miami's Little Havana, Boston's Irish Southie, and Los Angeles's Little Tokyo, Little Saigon, Koreatown, and Mexican East LA, to name only a few. Large numbers of German and Polish immigrants settled in the American Midwest; Minnesota attracted large numbers of Swedes and Norwegians, where they still dominate. Hamtramck, Michigan, grew as a center for Polish immigration, and Dearborn, Michigan, became a center for Arab immigration. Solvang, California, was settled by Danes; Fresno, California, attracted large numbers of Armenians; Praha (Prague), Texas, was settled by Czechs; Tarpon Springs, Florida, attracted a large Greek population; and the small town of Willimantic, Connecticut, now contains so many Puerto Ricans that locals sometimes call it Willirico.

Large concentrations of people allow the maintenance of the most diverse set of cultural communities. In New York City, for example, you can find more than 150 daily and weekly newspapers in languages from Russian to Bengali to Chinese to Hebrew. New York contains not only Spanish Harlem (which now contains a growing population from Mexico, in addition to Puerto Ricans) and Little Italy (which contains few Italians at this point), but dozens of cultural enclaves from the Hassidic community in Brooklyn's Borough Park and Crown Heights to the Irish-dominated Rockaway Park and Roxbury, the Russian-dominated Brighton Beach in Queens, and the West Indian–dominated Jamaica, all in Queens. In the Bronx, you'll find a concentration of Albanians in Belmont, Vietnamese and Cambodians in University Heights, and Jamaicans, Ecuadoreans, and Ghanaians in Tremont. London, England, contains an equivalent array of cultural communities, albeit biased to their former territories in the West Indies, Africa, Pakistan, India, and Bangladesh. France, likewise, contains Algerians, Moroccans, Libyan Arabs, and Senegalese. Germany contains enclaves of Turks, Greeks, Italians, Poles, Russians, Serbo-Croatians, and Spaniards.

Every country in the world contains communities that originated elsewhere. Although individuals have moved from one camp or village to another throughout the history of our species, most enclave communities date to the period just prior to, or subsequent to the Industrial Revolution. Within the last 200 years, Russians settled and left lasting influences in Harbin, China. The Portuguese did likewise in Macau, as did the British in Hong Kong and the English and American international settlement in Shanghai. Within the same time period, Lebanese created merchant communities throughout West Africa, as did Indians (who had been brought there initially as laborers) in East Africa, and as did Chinese merchants throughout Southeast Asia. Some enclave communities date to much earlier periods. The Jewish Diaspora created *shtetls* in Eastern Europe and Russia, ghettos in Western European cities, and around 800 years ago, religious communities in China, some of which, like that in Kaifeng, remain viable to this day.

The cultures of contemporary nation-states characteristically synthesize the cultures brought to them by immigrants. In his 1989 book *Albion's Seed*, for example, David Fischer suggests that whatever we might count as a distinctively American culture today came into being through the interaction among immigrants who brought to the New World four regional cultures from their homes in Britain. Puritans from East Anglia settled New England between 1629 and 1640; Cavaliers from south and west England settled Virginia and the adjacent Chesapeake Bay tidewater areas between 1642 and 1675; Quakers from England's North Midlands settled the Delaware Valley between 1675 and 1715; and migrants with origins in the regions north and south of the Scots-English border, some of whom first migrated to Northern Ireland, settled the American frontiers between 1717 and 1775. Fischer shows that each culture (like regional cultures everywhere) differed systematically in cultural assumptions and norms regarding speech, building styles, sex, marriage, children and family conventions, dress, religion, and foodways. Their root differences revolved about answers to the question: "Who best knows what choices are right for you?" Puritans answered "God, and those he has blessed with secular authority." Cavaliers answered "Me, but the more choices I have the more responsibility I have to treat others well and maintain my personal integrity." Quakers answered "Me, with guidance from the light within me; and because this is true for everyone, I extend to you and all people all the freedoms and liberties I want for myself." Migrants from the Scots-English borderlands answered "Me, and woe to anyone who says otherwise."

Puritans came to the New World, mostly from East Anglia's relatively privileged middle-class urban population, to build communities that mirrored Calvinist assumptions about the nature of God and humans. These hold that God alone rules all things, whereas humans, owing to Adam's fall from grace, are born depraved and unworthy, suitable only for eternal damnation. God's loving mercy, however, may provide for a person's salvation, as seen in that person's submission to God's rule and living according to God's moral law. But God may choose not to grant salvation. Human effort to submit to God's rule and live according to His moral law cannot produce salvation. Salvation comes only from submission to God's rule, which originates as a gift from God.

Communities modeled on this covenantal relationship between a single all-knowing and all-powerful authority and dependents expect submission to community norms, as did God in the covenants He

The Origin of Cultures

offered His creation. Community norm violations receive severe punishments that mirrored their importance, just as God punished Adam for his original sin by death—in Puritan Boston, this included the hanging of a number of Quakers who insisted on their own freedom of belief and speech. And community leaders took measures to protect some of their members from the consequences of chance events that threatened their well-being, just as God in His mercy grants some of Adam's descendants everlasting life. Puritans thus gave America a strain of collectivism and authoritarianism that vests rights in communities, not individuals, and attributes knowledge of what is best for community members to community leaders.

Cavaliers came from the upper layers of British society and, beginning with the English Civil War, brought with them indentured servants and an occasional slave to settle in Virginia and the adjacent Chesapeake Bay tidewater country. Part of this migration stream went first to Barbados, from which many emigrated subsequently into the Carolinas. In the New World, Cavaliers created communities organized hierarchically around themselves, the Church of England, and plantation agriculture. The latter re-created in the New World agricultural manors with traditions of servility and slavery, which originated in southern England 1,000 or so years earlier. "Can you trust that person?" constitutes a terribly important question in sharply stratified communities in which maintenance of the elite requires cooperation among its members. Moreover, the importance of the answer grows with a person's position in the local social hierarchy. In New World Cavalier communities, the most important answer to this question emerged as a construct of personal honor. An honorable man or woman is trustworthy by definition. Honorable people show it by treating others well, regardless of social position, by remaining faithful to their word and convictions and by consistently displaying personal honesty.

Cavaliers brought to the New World the idea that rights come to people by virtue of their birth and life circumstances. Freeborn people enjoy rights and freedoms merely because they are freeborn. But a person may lose their rights or increase them. The English Civil War taught Cavaliers that the best way to maintain their position meant avoiding dependency on government or other people. Cooperation among elite peers based on a code of personal honor most effectively maintained one's independence. Cavaliers thus gave America a strain of individualism and independence jealous of its privileges and hostile to local authority, founded on the cultural norm of personal integrity and kindness to others.

Quakers, mostly from modest social origins, both urban and rural, came mainly from the highlands of England's North Midlands, which had been settled primarily by Vikings prior to the Norman invasion. Founders of what came to be known as the Society of Friends broke away from Puritan groups when they substituted for Calvinist assumptions the claim that all individuals contain a "light within" which provides the means for the personal, direct experience of God. Quaker assumptions evolved from a line of logic that, we may imagine, ran something like this: Given that God may intervene in peoples' lives, it must be true that God may intervene in anyone's life. If that is true, everyone must have the capacity for direct, personal experience of God. If this is true, everyone must have something of God inside them. If this is true, everyone must have insights given by God. And if this is true, we should learn best by consulting with each other. Some people ("weighty friends") may have greater insight than others, but if we rule out some points of view we miss part of God's message. Therefore, we should listen to all, weigh our words and ideas, and work out agreements by consensus.

If we reason from the cultural assumption that all individuals contain a "light within," discrimination and inequalities imposed on any basis other than how well one treats another thus constitute wrongs. By implication, rights belong to individuals and everyone holds the same set—to believe and say and practice your beliefs, so long as they do not intrude on the rights of others; to a say in who exerts authority over you; and to freely participate in the exercise of community authority. These translate into protections against unwarranted taxation, property confiscation, speedy trials by a randomly selected jury of peers, with equal treatment for both prosecution and defense. Quakers thus gave America a strain of individualism founded on the cultural norm that the golden rule applies to everyone.

Migrants from the Scots-English border, both gentry and tenants, both small businessmen and highly skilled craftsmen and unskilled laborers and servants, learned from surviving in a region subject to continuous and horrific levels of violence for 700 years that men, too often, are evil and that governments cannot be trusted to protect you but they can be trusted to destroy you if you give them a chance. After arrival in the New World, they moved quickly beyond the coastal settlements into the frontier regions of the early colonial settlements, into the Appalachian mountain range from Maine to Georgia, and beyond, primarily into what became the American South and Southwest. Borderland migrants, proud of the skills that made them survivors, formed communities characterized by dispersed rather than nucleated settlements and leadership patterns modeled after families, where loyalties and trust follow from personal knowledge of specific people. Borderlands migrants thus gave America a strain of distrust of institutionalized authorities, reliance on trust based on personal knowledge of specific people, individualism highly sensitive to threats to personal well-being, and fast, aggressive responses to those threats with the most effective weapons available.

We Learn From Our Neighbors

The most recent female ancestor from whom all contemporary people descend, called Mitochondrial Eve because the mitochondrial DNA in all of us came from her, lived somewhere in northeast Africa about 100–200,000 years ago. The human population of that time may have been so small that everyone from whom all of us later descended spoke a single language and shared a single culture. Population growth and subsequent migration took their descendants to all parts of our planet. Some became farmers, others pastoralists, and a few remained foragers. Some of the farmers created civilizations and one of these initiated the industrial free-market revolution. Their subsequent histories produced relative isolation and divergent cultural evolution. Subsequent contact between these communities of long-separated relatives, primarily for trade and war, opened a flow of information about the new cultural things created out of the new sensory fields that the history of each had yielded. Loan words constitute one common outcome. English now contains words that originated in Arabic (tariff, magazine, jar, cotton, algebra, admiral), Chinese (tycoon, tea, silk, yen), various American Indian languages (caribou, caucus, chipmunk, moose, coyote, chocolate, cigar, potato, tomato), Indonesian languages (mango, sarong, compound, bamboo, cooties, batik), and African languages (OK, coffee, banana, jazz, gumbo, okra, yam), to cite only a few examples. The English word Coca-Cola now exists as a loan word in every language in the world. Ironically, and appropriately, the word consists of loan words from languages in South America (coca, probably from Quechua) and West Africa (cola).

Neighbors can teach us new and better ways to do things. They also help us differentiate between options that have consequences so shrouded in ambiguity that we can't tell if one choice really differs from another. Today, examples include what soft drink or laundry detergent or make of running shoe to buy or what politician to vote for. We may as well flip a coin. In lieu of coin-flipping, we pay attention to what other people say and do, perhaps especially those we admire. Celebrities hawk products of all kinds, from Nike shoes to car insurance to candidates for president. Celebrities, even if they consist only of an imaginary gecko, count as a kind of authority. An authority can help you avoid errors because he or she knows things that you do not, can use that knowledge to make decisions without your consent or input, and can ask you to do things. When an authority asks you to do something, you should do it, or at least seriously consider doing it.

A lifetime of experience in making errors leads us also to pay attention to the behavior of people we don't know and may have never met. In 2006, for example, Matthew Salganik, Peter Dodds, and Duncan Watts showed that among more than 14,000 teens exposed through an Internet experiment to a list of previously unknown songs by previously unknown bands, knowledge about previous downloads increased the popularity of the most popular songs and decreased the popularity of the least popular songs. Individuals make choices independent of their own evaluation based on what they see other people do, something we call an informational cascade. We engage in supportive behavior with others that produces an outcome that none of the participants wanted, something we call the Abilene Paradox after the example Jerry Harvey provided to illustrate his idea in 1974.

When ambiguity shrouds the consequences of alternatives, we act in ways that do not violate cultural norms because the one that remains counts as a threat. We call these things names: crowd behavior, groupthink, and peer pressure. If we find ourselves surrounded by a crowd of people running in the opposite direction from how we're heading, we turn around and run with them. In a Catholic or Anglican church service, we stand when others stand, kneel when others kneel, and bow our heads when others bow their heads. In a Methodist or Baptist service, we stand when others stand to sing a hymn, even if we don't sing along with them. Individual decisions may support existing cultural behavior patterns. They may also produce their own shared behavior, as in the experiment reported by Salganik, Dodds, and Watts, or as David Dalby noted in 1971, as in the processes through which the expression /o ke/, which was brought to America by Mande slaves born on the coast of West Africa, made its way into our language as OK, a word pronounced the same and with the same meaning as the original Mande word.

Kroeber and Kluckhohn made the point half a century ago that the neighbors from whom we learn need not be our contemporaries.

[A modern scholar who learns about mediaeval North African culture from Ibn Khaldun] . . . does not interact with the person, Ibn Khaldun, nor the latter's Muslim contemporaries. The modern scholar really encounters, through a book, a different way of life which (as filtered through his personality and culture) he then reacts to and tends to diffuse into his own culture. (1952:186)

Moreover, cultures may span many generations and many levels of human affairs. For example, Kroeber and Kluckhohn write: "Mohammedan culture, as we know it today, cuts across communities, societies, and nations. Roman society ceased to exist as such more than a millennium ago, but Roman culture was a vital force throughout the Middle Ages and, in certain aspects, is still 'alive' today" (1952:186). Even while it clearly draws from a broader Islamic culture, for example, the current global jihad differs significantly. Its differences are drawn, ironically, from broader non-Islamic and primarily Western cultures of warfare, finance, communication, and organization. Cultures consist of a set of things that hang together irrespective of where they originated. Jihadic culture, like all cultures, is made unique by the manner in which it organizes a configuration of shared cultural things that stands at the intersection of many broader cultures.

Ralph Linton made this point vividly in 1936. He tells us how an ordinary American citizen, who dresses in clothes modeled after garments created by nomads of the Central Asian steppes, begins his day. For breakfast he eats a version of cereal and milk, a practice that originated in the Southwest Asia and, perhaps, an egg from a species of bird domesticated in Southeast Asia together with strips of flesh from an animal domesticated in East Asia that had been salted and smoked by a process developed in Northern Europe. Linton ends with this (1936:327):

> When our friend has finished eating he settles back to smoke, an American Indian habit, consuming a plant domesticated in Brazil in either a pipe, derived from the Indians of Virginia, or a cigarette, derived from Mexico. If he is hearty enough he may even attempt a cigar, transmitted to use from the Antilles by way of Spain. While smoking he reads the news of the day, imprinted in characters invented by the ancient Semites upon a material invented in China by a process invented in Germany. As he absorbs the accounts of foreign troubles he will, if he is a good conservative citizen, thank a Hebrew deity in an Indo-European language that he is 100 per cent American.

The gunpowder in the bomb Ayat used to kill Rachel originated in China, the technology was developed in Western Europe, the martyrdom she sought goes back to early Syrian Christian thought with roots in ancient Jewish concepts (*Kiddush Hashem*), she was financed through Western institutions that developed in the Middle Ages, and the coordination of her behavior with fellow jihadists was facilitated with information technologies that originated in Bell Labs in the United States. The success of Ayat's attack thus rests, ironically, on products of the Western culture that the contemporary jihad-by-the-sword seeks to destroy.

Information Volume Regulates How Much We Learn

Variation in historical and regional context provides one set of choices to some people and a different set of choices to others and produces different historically and regionally specific cultures. Both Connecticut Yankees and Puerto Rican migrants to Connecticut, for example, bring to parenthood assumptions constructed from their experiences with family members, teachers, and friends, which may vary by birth cohort, gender, and specific social origins. Global movement of people, particularly toward the end of the 20th century, placed individuals who embodied different cultures face-to-face. But mass and instantaneous global communication has produced cultural merging. A successful rap group comes out of Japan; you can watch the movie *Slumdog Millionaire* in an African bush village; and Russians play jazz, compose country music, and turn capitalist. Because each of us learns from the sensory fields to which we have been exposed, when you first meet someone you can't easily tell by that person's age, gender, dress, or skin color which cultures you share and which you don't. Detecting cultural differences comes only from listening for the right cues—speech or other behavioral patterns that make no sense or which don't form part of your personal cultural repertoire. We can't tell from shared historical and regional origins alone, for example, whether Connecticut Yankee natives and Puerto Rican migrants use distinctive cultural models of what constitutes and how to organize a working relationship with their child's teacher.

Research I carried out a few years ago revealed two cultural models of parent-teacher cooperation. One set of parents and teachers took the view that parents had one set of responsibilities and teachers had another and that each contributed equally to a child's success in school. Another set of parents and teachers took the view that both parents and teachers shared the same set of responsibilities and should help each other help a child. These differences bear on the effectiveness of parent-teacher relationships in very important ways. A parent (teacher) who tries to create an effective working relationship based on the separate-but-equal model with a teacher (parent) who employs the mutual decision-makers model sets themselves up for the classic symptoms of clashing cultures—misunderstandings, disappointments, frustration—and an ineffective if not hostile parent-teacher relationship. A mother who employed the mutual decision-makers but who continually ran into teachers who employed the separate-but-equals model explained:

> I feel *super* strongly about this. I've given talks about it [to parent-teacher groups]! I really hated the ones [teachers] when you went

in to talk about your child and all they talked about was what *they* were doing in the classroom! I hated them to the degree that they eventually hated me. I just *wouldn't* give up.

But this cultural difference did not evolve from the historical and regional differences embodied in the labels for these parents and teachers. About half the separate-but-equal parents were Connecticut Yankee natives and half were Puerto Rican migrants. Likewise, about half the mutual decision-making parents were Connecticut Yankee natives and half were Puerto Rican migrants.

While writing the paper that reported these findings, I heard a National Public Radio report about type-casting and stereotypes in the entertainment industry. A Japanese American explained how he walked out of a casting session for a Japanese mobster after having been told repeatedly that his accent was wrong for the part, until he selected one that represented a stereotypical Cantonese Chinese. A Latina script-writer explained her successful writing career by reference to her non-Hispanic professional name. An African American actor and director explained how bias enters into the choices made by most of the people who control the industry because they have little or no historical experience with real people who have brown skin tones and minority ethnic labels. Increasingly, we find standing face-to-face with us people we might *think* embody different cultures, but who don't.

Populations that live primarily in ethnic enclaves today, however, undergo cultural change of the kind that produced the divergent cultural evolution characteristic of the descendants of Mitochondrial Eve. Unexpected cultural innovations arise and spread within that community and make it increasingly different from its cultural surroundings. The sources of enclave isolation may originate with the host population, the immigrant population, or some combination of the two. Growing differences make inevitable cultural conflict of the kind seen in the eruptions of jihad over the last few years in Madrid, London, Paris, Berlin, and elsewhere in Europe. Beyond this, and knowing that conflict resolution requires the merging of cultural differences, we know little about this increasingly prevalent and important issue.

Unimpeded interaction among different cultures, by contrast, facilitates the sharing of information and the sorting out of things that

The Origin of Cultures

work from things that work better. Characteristically, open interaction yields cultural synthesis. Elements from all four cultures brought to America by the earliest British colonists find expression, for example, in the U.S. Declaration of Independence as well as in the subsequent U.S. Constitution and Bill of Rights. Here's the core of the Declaration of Independence:

> We hold these truths to be self-evident, that all men are created equal, that they are endowed by their Creator with certain unalienable Rights, that among these are Life, Liberty and the pursuit of Happiness. — That to secure these rights, Governments are instituted among Men, deriving their just powers from the consent of the governed, — That whenever any Form of Government becomes destructive of these ends, it is the Right of the People to alter or to abolish it, and to institute new Government, laying its foundation on such principles and organizing its powers in such form, as to them shall seem most likely to effect their Safety and Happiness. Prudence, indeed, will dictate that Governments long established should not be changed for light and transient causes; and accordingly all experience hath shewn that mankind are more disposed to suffer, while evils are sufferable than to right themselves by abolishing the forms to which they are accustomed. But when a long train of abuses and usurpations, pursuing invariably the same Object evinces a design to reduce them under absolute Despotism, it is their right, it is their duty, to throw off such Government, and to provide new Guards for their future security.

Puritan culture provided the covenantal relationship between an all-powerful and all-knowing authority and dependents. Cavalier, Quaker, and borderlands cultures stood the Puritan version on its head to assign the status of all-powerful and all-knowing to people and dependency to government. Quaker culture provided the foundation for the central claim of the equality of all people and their shared unalienable rights. Cavalier and borderlands cultures contributed language that expresses jealousy over these rights, and distrust of government. Borderlands culture provided the norm of self-defense, and Cavalier culture transformed this norm into a duty, a matter of personal integrity (honor), to destroy tyrannical forms of government. By the mid-20th century, these assumptions had become integrated with indigenous cultural traditions in the Americas, Africa, the Middle East, and East Asia and had coalesced into human rights claims that warranted colonial independence. In 1948, this appeared formally as the United Nations Declaration of Universal Human Rights.

Two Rules for Cultural Design

Although the volume of information regulates how much we learn, the usefulness of the information regulates *what* we eventually learn. When we look closely at the cultures of foragers, pastoralists, and nonindustrialized farmers, it is as if each embodies a resource management design that provides for collective action to address specific sustainability problems. These elegantly simple designs reflect just two rules—do nothing you don't have to, but all you can to improve your material well-being.

The Shoshone of North America's Great Basin, the San who live in the Kalahari, and the Mbuti Pygmies of the Congo rainforest share a strategic problem, for example: an inability to control the location and timing of a relatively small food supply stream. If too many people live at the same location and consume the available food too quickly, or if they don't move to the available food when and where it's available, they won't survive for long. Foragers thus must live in small, mobile camps. It doesn't pay to build elaborate houses or to lay claims to land. Cultural rules of local group exogamy require people to establish visiting patterns between camps, force people to move from the camp in which they grew up, and thus create a safety network of family ties over a broad landscape. The absence of cultural rules that restrict camp membership facilitates movement when needed, and a bilateral mode of identifying family members maximizes the number of camps in which one might move in an emergency.

Excellence—in tracking, arrow point production, knowledge of the location of root vegetables—brought prestige and admiration, but nearly everyone did something well and no one performed most things well. Men hunted, but in most foraging communities women gathered most of the food eaten. Sharing constituted a critically important norm because no one could count on being able to support themselves solely by themselves for any length of time. Men hunt because family continuity depends on the women who produce the

The Origin of Cultures

children. Placing women at risk would be foolhardy. Eskimo (called Inuit in Canada) women experience inequalities with men that their peers in Australia or the Kalahari do not. The foraging cultures of the American Pacific Northwest exhibit significant intracommunity ranking and inequalities. These exceptions to the prevailing patterns of foraging populations conform to the exceptional circumstances of the peoples who live in the American Arctic and Pacific Northwest. The rarity of significant plant food in the Arctic meant that Eskimo depended for their survival on men's hunting skills. The reliable runs of salmon into the rivers of the Pacific Northwest meant that it paid to create property rights.

Likewise, Fulani, Maasai, and Kazak pastoralists share a similar strategic problem that differs from the one faced by foragers, just slightly—an inability to control the location and timing of a relatively small food supply stream for their animals. Pastoralist cultures emerged on the periphery of centers of food domestication in regions too dry to support rain-fed agriculture but with sufficient rain to support grasslands on which cattle, goats, sheep, camels, and equivalent animals could graze. To sustain a family herding animals requires one to have many, many animals and in these semi-arid regions each animal needs access to a large amount of grazing land. If too many animals live at the same location and consume the available food too quickly or if they don't move to the available food when and where it's available, they won't survive for long. Pastoralists, like foragers, thus must live in small, mobile camps. Unlike most foragers, however, pastoralists created property rights and organized themselves so they could assemble huge numbers of people for concerted action.

Cattle produce more cattle, and sheep produce more sheep. By producing more of themselves, these sources of food thus constitute a stream of income. Unlike wild animals and plants, domesticated animals become wealth. Foragers generally do not lay claim to land or animals or plants because the uncertainties of a food supply stream made claiming just one part of the landscape foolish. Pastoralists lay claim to their animals because they constitute a relatively certain food supply stream. Because this form of wealth moves itself, however, it is highly susceptible to theft. Men defend the herds because family size and strength depends on the women who produce the children.

Pastoralists, like foragers, shield their women from foolish risks. Men's defense of herds gives them an investment of time and energy that warrants their ownership claim. Men want their brothers and sons to help with defense because they know them better than they know other men. The sets of brothers and their sons that defend herds maintained by a pattern of patrilocal residence at marriage are extended by the passage of animals from fathers to sons, which gives emphasis to a line of patrilineal descent. The common interest of sets of brothers and their sons warrants the emergence of a family corporation in which all members hold joint title to a common set of property.

Within this context, the brother of a deceased man may serve as the living embodiment of his ghost, marry and bear children in the brother's name, and thus perpetuate an important line of descent. Similarly, a barren woman may assume the position of a man, marry a woman who bears children in her name, and thus add to the manpower of her patrilineal family. Within farming communities, ghost marriages offer a solution to the similar problem of family continuity. In many areas of West Africa, daughters assumed the social position and activities of sons to solve the same problem. Women who lived in West African states might grow quite wealthy as merchants. Some assumed the social position and activities of a husband to maintain their wealth within their patrilineal family line. Ghost marriages and female husbands thus make perfect sense.

Farmers, too, share a common strategic problem that sets them apart from pastoralists—access to sufficient amounts of land and labor of the right kind at the right time. Moreover, farmers had no choice but to live in permanent settlements. Permanent settlement created four new problems that mobile groups never had to face. First, to farm meant that you had to clear brush and forest so you could plant crops. This destroyed wild game habitat. Habitat destruction together with the presence of a settled population rapidly depleted game reserves. As their supply of protein diminished farming populations began to encounter nutritional disease, particularly protein-calorie malnutrition. Second, permanent settlements created a problem of waste disposal and, thus, diarrheal disease. Third, permanent settlements meant congestion, which created conditions suitable for the spread of respiratory disease. Finally, landscape changes near permanent settlements often created breeding grounds for mosquitoes, which served as carriers of diseases like malaria and yellow fever. Population growth intensified these health problems and death rates rose. Birth rates rose, too, if for no other reason than the increased time men and women spent with each other compared with the separations imposed when men left camp to hunt or to lead herds to fresh pasture. Very high birth and death rates created populations with even more children and even fewer very old people than in foraging or pastoral communities. Death was a very common occurrence, and elders gained respect not only as repositors of critically important knowledge but also for their rarity.

For the earliest farmers, land was free, as it has been among contemporary farming populations where population density has remained very low. Population growth, however, created conflicts over land within walking distance of a settlement. A common response was to move. At some point, however, it makes more sense to fight for land than to move. Farmers lay claim to land like pastoralists lay claim to animals because it makes possible a relatively certain food supply stream. Men defend the land because family size and strength depends on the women who produce the children. Placing women at risk would be foolhardy. Men's defense of land gives them an investment of time and energy that warrants their ownership claim. Men want their brothers and sons to help with defense because they know them better than they know other men. The sets of brothers and their sons who defend land maintained by a pattern of patrilocal residence at marriage is extended by the passage of land from fathers to sons, which gives emphasis to a line of patrilineal descent. The common interest of sets of brothers and their sons warrants the emergence of a family corporation in which all members hold joint title to a common set of property.

In some regions of expanding populations, such as in a broad band just south of the Congo River basis that stretches from the west to the east coast of Africa, fighting took men away from their families. The women who had to take over the farm work wanted to work with their sisters and daughters because they knew them better than they knew other women. The sets of sisters and their daughters that worked the land encouraged a pattern of matrilocal residence at marriage. Common residence was extended by the passage of land from mothers to daughters, which gives emphasis to a line of matrilineal descent. The common interest of sets of sisters and their daughters warrants the emergence of a family corporation in which all members hold joint title to a common set of property. Most commonly, when the men returned home they assumed responsibility for land management, which often led to a shift in which men brought their wives to live near their mother's brother.

Wherever you look, you'll see cultural patterns consistent with the rules "Do nothing you don't have to but all you can to improve your material well-being." These include patterns as prosaic as paths worn into lawns when sidewalk placement fails to correspond with minimum distances between travel points, and patterns that signal fundamental global cultural changes like the phenomenal growth of Web commerce, which rose from $31 billion in retail sales in 2001 to $175 billion in 2007 and, according to Forrester.com, may reach $335 billion by 2012. Similarly, Ayat's murder-suicide illustrates a cultural pattern of warfighting used commonly by weak opponents to inflict on powerful enemies maximal damage for minimum cost. Ayat and Rachel went to the supermarket because these institutions integrate a large number of economic functions at a single location and thus provide maximal shopping opportunities for minimum cost. The same principles explain the relative size and location of all kinds of central places, including the choice of the World Trade Center and the Pentagon as targets of the 9/11 attacks.

Cultural Dynamics

The ways in which our brains store and process information in sensory fields means that individually unique life trajectories yield individually unique people whose choices direct the course of their lives. New things only come from the minds of particular people at particular times. Critically important sensory input comes to us in the form of other people's behavior, however. Over the course of our lives and through various means—listening to news reports, reading, traveling, talking with friends or family members, taking courses or attending workshops, or explicit and rigorous research—we come to think differently about the components of our world. We think of new ways to organize activities and new ways to think about domains of understanding. By interacting with other people—acting and responding to what we experience of other people's words and acts—we actively participate in an unceasing process that leads to changes in assumptions, the norms that come from these assumptions, and how we act, and produces the shared understandings and patterns of behavior visible in the patterned, repetitive behavior that makes culture seem like a thing.

Our cognitive and behavioral response to that input reflects our prior life history and the personal configuration of assumptions, norms, and behavior that our minds construct from that history of experience. This produces evolutionary change in cultures. We build on our past and shape the future with it. This implies that what exists now could not exist without what went before and what exists now sets limits to what can come next.

Our behavioral responses elicit reciprocal cognitive, emotional, and behavioral responses from others. We call this social interaction. Other people influence us and constrain what we think and do by means of their behavior—by what they do or don't do, by the circumstances of their life, as well as by their immediate responses to our responses; we influence others likewise. By virtue of the sensory input it generates, social interaction and living our lives in the presence of others thus reciprocally produces evolution in the cultures that we use to live our lives.

The *recurrent, patterned* behavior that characterizes a culture exhibits the properties of a thing because recurrent behavior constitutes an environment in which we carry out daily activities and which elicits cognitive, emotional, and behavioral responses. In eliciting these responses, recurrent, patterned behavior thus elicits evolution in the configuration of culture our mind uses to produce personal cognitive, emotional, and behavioral responses to input from the sensory fields to which we become exposed later. Certain forms of recurrent, patterned behavior (e.g., those that produce childhood traumatic stress) may induce specific, lifelong changes in how our minds work and in the behavioral trajectory of our lives.

But all this says is that new things come into being all the time, unexpectedly, and contribute to an ongoing evolution of culture that takes shape as people interact with each other. That identifies the source of new things, why we can't predict them, why each builds on predecessors, and the immediate social context of cultural evolution. But it doesn't explain why we select specific new things and not others in ways that, in retrospect, make perfect sense. It doesn't explain why we select the specific new things that make our lives better. *Recurrent, patterned* behavior means that people with whom we interact make patterned choices from among the alternatives they see. *Patterned choices* come from the application of specific criteria to the choice alternatives provided by sensory input. Our minds rationalize *recurrent, patterned* responses in the form of domain-specific theories, models, or schemas, which consist of assumptions about the nature, components, and both the instrumental and moral organization of the world of sensory experience. In the next chapter, I argue that we manage to transform the chaos, error, and ambiguities of the present into retrospective rationality and continually do things better because evolved choice mechanisms direct us to learn some things but not others.

Selected Bibliography

Dalby, D. (1971). O.K., A.O.K. and O KE. *New York Times*, January 5, pp. L-31/4-6.

Fischer, D.H. (1989). *Albion's seed: Four British folkways in America.* New York: Oxford University Press.

Fuentes C. (2008). Pathways from interpersonal violence to sexually transmitted infections: A mixed-method study of diverse women. *Journal of Women's Health,* 17, 1591–1603.

Handwerker, W.P. (2002). The construct validity of cultures: Culture theory, cultural diversity, and a method for ethnography. *American Anthropologist,* 104, 106–122.

Harvey, J.B. (1974). The Abilene paradox and other meditations on management. *Organizational Dynamics,* 3, 63–80.

Kroeber, A.L. & Kluckhohn, C. (1952). *Culture: A critical review of concepts and definitions.* New York: Vintage Books.

Linton, R. (1936). *The study of man.* New York: Appleton Century Crofts.

Salganick, M.J., Dodds, P.S., & Watts, D.J. (2006). Experimental study of inequality and unpredictability in an artificial cultural market. *Science,* 311, 854–856.

Zipf, G.K. (1949). *Human behavior and the principle of least effort.* Cambridge, MA: Addison-Wesley.

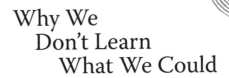

Why We
Don't Learn
What We Could

I learned the following things and I bet you did, too:

- People can eat fish, chickens, and cattle.

- People can walk down the road, run, and dance.

- People cannot thrive well when they drink gasoline and eat plastic.

- People cannot leap off tall buildings and soar like birds into the clouds.

I learned some of these things, but you may have learned others:

- People can eat dirt, ants, grubs, pigs, horses, and dogs.

- Witches can transform themselves into creatures that fly through the night.

- Warriors should not target noncombatants.

- People who reject Islam should be killed.

I learned none of these things and I doubt you did either:

- People cannot eat fish, chickens, and cattle.

- People cannot walk down the road, run, and dance.

- People can thrive well when they drink gasoline and eat plastic.

- People can leap off tall buildings and soar like birds into the clouds.

What distinguishes these different kinds of things?

The simple answer is: clarity of evidence. Consequences make a thing bad or good. Bad things do us harm. Really bad things kill us. Really good things transform our life in wondrous ways. Some things aren't really bad or good, except in particular circumstances or due to idiosyncratic whim, so beyond those concerns it doesn't matter whether we learn them or not. Things that we could learn and did learn are things that have a large balance of good-to-bad consequences. Things that we could learn and some did and some did not learn are of things that have either bad consequences in some historical situations and good consequences in others or have no consequence worth mentioning. Things that we could learn and did not are things that have a large balance of bad-to-good consequences.

Why We Tell Good from Bad

The difference between good and bad may mean the difference between life and death or, if not that, then the difference between a miserable life and a better one. The living things that don't pay attention to the difference between good and bad don't last long, if they ever existed at all. Useful information distinguishes reliably between the two. Living things that don't eat well reliably die quickly. Dead things can't reproduce. If they reproduced before they died, they can't contribute to the survival and subsequent reproduction of their offspring. This isn't important to species like Pacific salmon, which reproduce and die long before their fertilized eggs hatch. But species whose continuity from one generation to the other requires creative learning of the kind outlined in Chapter 2 must distinguish good from bad reliably, or perish.

Think, for example, about the food on which living things depend and the times and places living things can acquire it—for short, let's call these things resources. If resources change in ways that living things can't track, they die. Tracking mechanisms that induced change as an automatic response to specific forms of information without integrating information from different sensory fields would work fine, so long as resources changed slowly relative to the length of a generation. More rapid resource change, however, would call for a tracking mechanism that induced change by integrating stored with current sensory information so the creature could change its behavior effectively during its own lifetime. Thus, if the length of a generation grows relative to significant resource changes, the only kinds of living things that would survive would be those which had evolved some form of simple learning. These creatures would possess a resource-tracking mechanism that perceived and stored physical properties of a sensory field, perhaps in individual neurons, identified poor correspondences between perceptions and memories of resources, and induced appropriate forms of behavioral change.

Simple forms of learning alone, however, would kill creatures exposed to resource changes that occurred often and unpredictably over its lifetime. Resource changes of this sort call for a tracking mechanism like the one described in Chapter 2, in which the mind perceives and stores properties of sensory fields as coded firing patterns. Coded firing patterns construct ideas and behavior creatively. Coded firing patterns also generate mistakes, of course. If that's all that evolved in our ancestors, we wouldn't be here. Learning depends on mistake correction. Moreover, our ancestors had evolved a cultural environment that changed increasingly rapidly and that demanded that they learn increasing amounts of information. This meant that they had to rectify their mistakes increasingly rapidly. Specifically, mistake correction must give us clues about how to avoid death, eat well reliably, and reproduce. Trial-and-error learning winnows out the errors and leaves us with the useful information that increases our chances of avoiding death, eating well reliably, and reproducing.

Winnowing the Good from the Bad

Learning tasks that come with few options rarely produce error. Members of a recent graduate seminar on Cultural Dynamics offered two excellent examples. One member pointed out that he once swore in front of his mother, but did so only that one time because she became so angry. Another pointed out that she never made that mistake because she saw what happened to *her* brother when he made it.

Tasks that entail more than two choices, between "do it" or "don't do it," characteristically produce mistakes that grow in number with the choices you have to make to accomplish the task. Writing provides an important and simple example. It's important because the emergence of writing vastly expanded the collective memory that the evolution of language had made possible in the first place and quickened the pace of cultural evolution. It's important also because learning to write provides an example of the purest form of social learning. Writing, like language and money, is institutionalized in widely agreed on assumptions about what counts as good writing, what counts as bad, and when and how to write something badly so that it counts as good (epitomized, perhaps, by William Faulkner's never-ending sentences).

A set of norms follow from these assumptions that tell us how we should write. We should write active verbs in concise sentences. We should use "that" when we refer to a class of things and reserve "which" to refer to a specific thing or set of things. We should summarize in the same tense. We should place things we want to emphasize at the end of sentences. We should provide transitions from one paragraph to another and from one chapter to another. We should make sure that we coordinate what we say at the beginning with what we say at end of our story. We learn to write from authorities like Strunk and White's *The Elements of Style*, authors whose writing we admire, and elementary, high school, and college teachers. Writing makes a simple example because every reader of this book also writes. Think back about how you learned to write and you'll see that even the purest forms of social learning can't be accomplished without lots of individual trial-and-error learning.

Some of you write well and others don't. Whether you write well or not, the chances are good that you write better now than you did as a child, unless you haven't written in a long time. It's hard to keep all the rules of good writing in mind and let them come through your fingertips; that takes practice, more practice, and still more practice. And the practice won't go anywhere unless you or another reader finds the mistakes you make. You acquired many if not most of those rules with help. Someone, perhaps many people over time, corrected how you assembled characters into properly spelled words, words into sentences, and sentences into paragraphs, and paragraphs into essays, articles, chapters, or books. You also learned by absorbing the implicit rules in the writing of the authors that you enjoy reading. If you sit down to write right now, the words, sentences, and paragraphs that come through your fingertips will not read superbly, even if your words, sentences, and paragraphs serve your immediate purpose just fine.

You can improve your writing with reflection and with the help of someone who helps you find better ways to tell your story. The best writers ordinarily rewrite and rewrite and rewrite and rewrite still more. Each step winnows the chaff and improves the readability of your story. Those of you who play games seriously know personally that playing well, like writing well, takes practice and more practice and more practice and still more practice. You also know that a coach who helps you find your mistakes makes for better improvement than practice without a coach. The very best athletes, like Michael Jordan or Diana Taurasi, Tiger Woods or Anneka Sorenstam, Emmitt Smith, or Mia Hamm, don't achieve greatness without it.

Winnowing Makes for Incremental Change

The observations that some of us write well and others don't and that some of us play games well and others don't tell us that all human populations contain people who vary in what and how well they learned one thing or another. All communities thus contain variations on cultural themes. Some work poorly, others work acceptably, and still others work superbly. In Wikipedia, the online encyclopedia open to all for editorial contributions and corrections, it's easy to see how winnowing by an Army of Davids (to borrow Glenn Reynolds's phrase) separates the good from the bad to produce incremental changes that systematically improve articles on millions of different topics. Likewise, it's easy to imagine how winnowing separated the good from the bad to produce incremental changes that created even the biggest events in our history, like the agricultural revolution.

Winnowing starts with a problem. A problem means that things don't work right, or not as well as we think they should. The mistakes our minds produce mean that problems don't elicit their solutions. But as Homer Barnett pointed out 50 years ago, a problem draws attention to the importance of new things, activates a search for solutions, and heightens awareness of novelty. At least some of the things needed for an effective solution may already exist as variations within a community's cultural inventory.

Hand-axes, for example, likely started as a chipped stone. A hand-axe is a stone implement that first appears in human history some 1.5 million years ago but which remained as part of human tool kits until around 50,000 years ago. Wherever we find them, in Africa, Europe, or Asia, hand-axes exhibit the same form. A hand-axe is relatively flat, with the approximate dimensions of a man's hand (a breadth-to-length ratio of .618, which the ancient Greeks called the Golden Rectangle), and exhibits a sharpened edge around its entire pear-like shape. The hand-axe, with a cutting edge some four times greater than earlier cobble tools, constitutes one of the first examples of the human proclivity to adopt changes that improved productivity. Once you figure out how to give stones a sharp edge, it doesn't take much imagination to figure out how to systematically shape an entire rock. All you need is the incentive. William Calvin suggests that the incentive was something like a herd of antelope around a waterhole. The herd would offer an important form of food, but one that would likely spook if approached too closely. A rock thrown into the herd might induce pain sufficient to elicit a sitting response from an animal and, thus, give a hunter time to run up and kill it at close range. But how could you reliably hit animals and induce the kind of pain that elicits a sitting response? Calvin argues that the answer to this question doesn't require a neuroscientist. The original skills may well have been lost often and rediscovered just as often over the course of 1.5 million years. He may be right. But that doesn't mean that the answer is obvious even to a neuroscientist.

Increasing the edge of an existing cobble tool might increase the likelihood of inducing sufficient pain. Chipping off extraneous material would flatten the stone and make it possible to throw it farther and with more accuracy. Making a pear shape with the dimensions that approximate those of a man's hand would have improved a person's ability to grip the stone securely and added more accuracy. Even if we know how to chip stones, it isn't obvious that these three changes would produce a tool that effectively solved an important problem faced by our ancestors. Winnowing, however, would reveal the answer. Winnowing takes place when people trade ideas and techniques each works out through creative thinking and trial and error about how to chip stone in one way or another and which combinations of shape and sharpness work best.

Winnowing through the variants and errors produced by lots of people over many years reveals increasingly effective solutions to specific problems. The creation and use of the first stone tools would have made it easier to shape digging sticks with which to extract roots, to cut branches with which to build shelters, to kill, carve up and dismember game, and to protect oneself and one's food from competitors. The later use of fire made it possible to harden wood in ways that created more efficient and durable digging sticks and lances, to occupy colder regions, to cook food, and to protect oneself and one's food from competitors. The ability to harden wood made it possible to kill game more efficiently and improved stone tool design made it possible to carve up and dismember game more efficiently. The ability to cook food profoundly transformed both the reliability and the quality of the nutritional base of our ancestors. Cooking improved the nutritional value of meat because it reduced the likelihood of acquiring worms, which would have been common when meat was not cooked before it was eaten. Cooking increased the nutritional quality of the diet by making essential nutrients more readily available. Finally, cooking made it possible for people to use a vast range of new vegetable resources which, uncooked, had been indigestible or even poisonous. A sense of community and interdependence among people who hunted, cooked, and lived together would yield more effective cooperation and increasingly efficient production, reduced infant, child and maternal mortality, and more effective defense. Campfires extended the length of time our ancestors could carry out both work and social activities. They also provided a community focus for both, which contributed to the spread of information, enhanced the importance of communication, and quickened winnowing processes.

Changes like these improved our foraging ancestors' ability to survive, eat well reliably, and reproduce a new generation. The historical record clearly reveals incremental change that plausibly comes from such winnowing whenever we have enough data, as in the extraordinary sequence from the Tehuacan Valley in Mexico. As the archaeologist Richard MacNeish reported in 1978, in the centuries before 10,000 years ago, the people who lived in the Tehuacan Valley lived as mobile foragers who hunted horses, antelope, deer, and, perhaps, mammoths. They also hunted rabbits and collected seeds and fruit, but vegetable foods and small game comprised a very small segment of the diet. Beginning around 10,000 years ago, however, large game disappeared, possibly because a slight climatic warming reduced the available grassland. Subsequently, new technologies that built on preexisting technologies and were integrated with them allowed for the capture of small game and the harvest of plants. The dietary importance of vegetable foods grew. MacNeish notes that major improvements in productivity may have followed merely from more selective culling of grass seeds, more optimal camp locations, or a single woman's innovation at a propitious time—to wit: the Mesoamerican artisan who first came up with a way to weave baskets so tightly that they lost few or no seeds on the way back to camp and an increasingly dry climate at the end of the last Ice Age. This basketry-weaving innovation may have originated long before the climate change that made it important and set it apart from other ways in which women of the Tehuacan Valley wove baskets. Jointly, however, they made it both profitable and feasible to exploit seed resources and initiated the first step toward the origin of agriculture. By about 7,000 years ago, seasonal seed planting had begun to take place.

Over the succeeding 1,600 years, systematic use and selection of some of these plants led to their domestication. Domestication refers to the outcome of humanly directed biological evolution. Rather than plant the seeds of all plants, people plant the seeds from selected plants. When we selectively plant seeds from the plants that produced the largest number of seeds and from the plants that produce good-tasting seeds that are easier to convert into a tasty meal, over many plant generations we change the plant's genome in ways that yield new species of plants. This, too, consists of winnowing.

However, as late as 4,300 years ago, the economy of these people was scheduled seasonally as a mix of hunting (in the winter), seed collecting (in the spring and summer), and simple agriculture (in the summer and fall). During the succeeding 800 years, pottery made its first appearance. But it is not until 3,500 years ago that Mesoamericans produced enough food by agriculture to support themselves in permanent villages throughout the year. The agricultural revolution in Mesoamerica thus took some 5,100 years, about 110 times longer than it took England to launch the Industrial Revolution between 1780 and 1830.

Humans, meaning both you and me and the ancestors of both of us, come with minds that think creatively and make choices that seem to be the best, given our knowledge of the circumstances that exist when we make a choice. Then we try to correct our mistakes. In retrospect, our choices look patterned because they were subject to

The Origin of Cultures

selective winnowing. Because winnowing gives precedence to avoiding death, eating well reliably, and reproducing, when we look back at our collective history we see a clear directional trend toward increasing levels of productivity. When we look back to compare how foragers, pastoralists, and farmers live, it's as if they designed their cultures for the different circumstances each faced to minimize energy expenditure and maximize energy capture.

How We Tell Good from Bad

To move beyond storytelling, however, we have to identify more precisely the means by which we make such choices. Once we do, we can imagine the consequences and ask how those expectations fit the observations we make. Any good candidate for en evolved choice-making mechanism must induce behavior. Emotions do just that. In 1980, Robert Plutchik proposed eight basic emotions (acceptance, anger, anticipation, disgust, joy, fear, sadness, and surprise), which, in various combinations, produce the wide range of emotions that we experience; he argued that emotions evolved because they allowed quick recognition of events and contingencies that bear on our survival. Emotions evoke behavior. They not only allow for recognition of threats or opportunities, they goad us to respond. Highly selective construction of culture occurs because, like other creatures, we have brains that respond sensitively to environmental variations that bear on our ability to avoid predation and exploitation, eat well reliably, and reproduce.

The seminal work early in the 20th century by Walter Cannon and later in the century by Hans Selye envisioned stressors and stress responses as essential to life and living as breathing and beating hearts. Subsequent work, however, defined stressors as whatever evokes a stress response and imagined them as out-of-the-ordinary (acute or chronic) events. A bit more imagination suggests a far broader set of stressors, adds a set of supports, and yields a much more important role for stress. Stress signals both error and opportunity and, by its effects on our minds and bodies, induces specific choices that optimize our ability to avoid predation and exploitation, eat well reliably, and reproduce (see Box 4.1). Stress thus provides for the genesis of cultural difference and, thus, the specific forms of behavior that result

BOX 4.1. How Emotional Weights Get Assigned to Choices

Stress effects originate in complex interdependencies among what is called the hypothalamus-pituitary-adrenal (HPA) axis, the amygdala/hippocampal complex, and the prefrontal cortex. The first two parts belong to a part of our brains that first appeared hundreds of thousands of years ago called the limbic system. The limbic system controls our emotions, long-term memory formation, associations between emotions and experiences, and decision-making. The prefrontal cortex belongs to the more recently evolved part of our brains that we call the cerebral cortex, forms the back part of our frontal lobe, and constitutes the operational center of our minds' ability to plan, evaluate options, and coordinate ideas and actions. The information that elicits stress responses passes through the thalamus to the amygdala and, from there, to other part of the brain. The HPA system inhibits one part of the autonomic nervous system (the parasympathetic) and enhances the other (the sympathetic), which shuts down energy storage, reproductive, and growth functions, and increases the distribution and immediate availability of fuel to our brain as well as body. Glucocorticoids released from the adrenal gland enhance the long-term potentiation of hippocampal neurons and, like epinephrine released into the sympathetic nervous system, increase the brain's fuel supply by enhancing glucose uptake. Serotonin appears to activate noradrenergic neurons and contributes to the release of corticotrophic-releasing hormone (CRH), which controls the flow of glucocorticoids. Serotonin also induces long-lasting increases in the number of glucocorticoid receptors in hippocampal neurons.

Greater numbers of receptors means more finely tuned hippocampal detection of circulating glucocorticoids and feedback inhibition. The amygdala releases dopamine and norepinephrin, which, with serotonin, enhances its function, particularly the encoding of declarative and explicit memory mediated by hippocampal structures. Amygdala/hippocampal involvement thus induces effective encoding, and later retrieval, of memories with emotional weights. The amygdala also induces increased catecholamine release in the prefrontal cortex, which yields deficits in working memory. Supports, by contrast, appear to enhance prefrontal cortex control of behavior through as yet unspecified mechanisms. Possibly by lowering serotonin re-uptake, supports may enhance hippocampal control over circulating glucocorticoids.

in cultural evolution. Because the stress mechanism responds to both opportunity and error, it organizes our emotions in ways that yield the selective processes that lead us to correct initial choices revealed later as errors, to winnow the chaff. Because they bear differentially on well-being, stressors that reduce and increase well-being should exhibit effects sufficiently different to warrant different names—stressors and supports, respectively. Stressors include any form of uncertainty, like the inconsistencies between thought and action known under the name cognitive dissonance. Supports include any form of certainty, like the process of dissonance reduction, which yields consistency between thought and action.

We experience stressors and supports, respectively, as fear (and related emotions) and joy (and related emotions). During stress, attention increases and thus becomes more focused, even in the absence of awareness. Stress thus enhances our mind's abilities to identify, respond to an opportunity or threat optimally, and store pertinent declarative and habitual memories. Working memory may suffer deficits. But long-term memory tends to be encoded particularly effectively. Effective memory encoding enhances our ability to successfully anticipate and avoid, respond to, or take advantage of equivalent future opportunities or threats.

The strength and character of stress responses assigns emotional weights (made conscious and rationalized as costs and benefits) to choice alternatives by reference to variation in four key properties of the choices before us: (1) degree of threat or opportunity; (2) whether it bears on one's ability to avoid predation or exploitation, eat well reliably, or reproduce; (3) time for response; and (4) uncertainty of outcome. Stress responses exhibit their highest intensity when the threat or opportunity is great relative to any alternative, bears on one's ability to avoid predation or exploitation, requires an immediate response, and the outcome is highly uncertain. Increasing response times yield corresponding greater prefrontal cortex control of behavior and more measured responses. With long response times, the presence of competing stressors or opportunities redirects stress and may account for Parkinson's Law—our propensity to allow tasks to fill the time we have to complete them.

By assigning emotional weights to stressors and supports, stress induces choices that correspond with the difference in weights.

Increasing weight differences should correspond with increasing probabilities that people choose the alternative with the greatest weight. We experience freedom of choice when all members of a set of alternatives bear equal weights. In these circumstances, the probability of choosing any one alternative should equal the probability of choosing any other alternative. Panic may ensue when we face two choices that kill us. But the probability of choice still should approximate 50/50.

What This Means

Two features of the mind each of us is born with, both of which may have evolved hundreds of millions of years ago, make cultural evolution inevitable and direct the course of that evolution by reference to specific criteria. One feature of our mind produces a continuous flow of conceptual and behavioral variation and, thus, produces choice alternatives. The other feature assigns emotional weights to the consequences of choice alternatives. These emotional weights, which in consciousness appear rationalized as costs and benefits, determine the likelihood that you, or I, or any specific person, will choose one alternative rather than the other. This last feature of our minds thus constitutes a selective mechanism responsible for the production of new or the maintenance or change of preexisting patterns of behavior. We differentiate alternatives by their costs relative to their potential benefits. The presence and intensity of selective pressures thus may be measured as cost differentials.

Because each of us makes mistakes and because the world around us changes, a perfect culture can't exist. There's always a better way to look at the world and a better way to act. Knowledge and behavior may produce useful results for specific sets of circumstances. But the same knowledge and behavior may produce less than useful, perhaps self-destructive, results if circumstances change. Because our minds produce new things and select those that prove useful, changes in living circumstances produce changes in what people do and believe. Faced with alternatives, our minds tell us to act on the one that most likely maintains or improves our ability to survive, eat well reliably, and reproduce. This means the one by which we gain the most or lose the least—and this may occur even when we are not conscious of doing so.

Alternatives that cannot be differentiated in cost are selectively neutral. Neither alternative may reduce or improve our well-being, or both (or all) alternatives may reduce or improve our well-being by equal amounts. People are free to choose among alternatives like these on highly personal and even whimsical grounds. Indeed, genuine "freedom of choice" exists *only* when you can choose among selectively neutral alternatives. The position that all things possess the same moral standing, called ethical relativism, occurs as a viable choice almost solely among people who cannot seriously conceive that they might be battered, demeaned, raped, mutilated, or killed. The personal cost to a suicide bomber like Ayat may appear equivalent to, perhaps even less than, the cost of slower forms of death she faces having grown up in a culture in which, as Phyllis Chesler noted in her July 28, 2008, Chesler Chronicles blog entry, "being born female is often a capital crime, ... in which girls and women are honor murdered for the slightest, alleged infringements of the patriarchal rules."

Cost differences between alternatives constrain your freedom to choose and agency doesn't exist when you have no choice. Stress thus induces highly specific forms of learning that provides the genesis of cultural evolution. The blogger Grim at *Blackfive* wrote November 16, 2007, for example, that what we call PTSD (post-traumatic stress disorder):

> is not just about *combat*, but about reality. That's important to know, because it reinforces the point that this [PTSD] isn't something in you that has broken. It's just that you've learned something others haven't realized. Those lessons come from the world we live in, and point to its real nature. As such, the lessons can come from any place, anywhere the walls break down.

Walls break down most commonly, perhaps, in the gratuitous and exploitative sexual, physical, and emotional violence we try to sanitize with names like "interpersonal violence," or IPV. People who grow up in such traumatic/violent (exploitative) cultural environments learn to be highly sensitive to power relations, respond quickly and strongly when others attempt to take advantage of them, and, to minimize the chance of further exploitation, search harder than others for ways to avoid dependency. People subject to violence-induced learning thus confront radical cultural differences when they interact with people who, in Grim's words, "have never looked death in the eye, and never felt what it feels like to want to kill, or the guilt that comes from having wanted it." PTSD thus plausibly constitutes an evolved response to danger in which a person generalizes observations about the things in the world that may do you great damage. "Healing" from such trauma may require learning to distinguish the things that do from the things that do not pose a danger. This, Danielle Wozniak suggests, may come only with successful movement through the liminality stage of the rite-of-passage that allows reintegration into a wider cultural community.

Intense selection pressure makes for cultural uniformity. Little or no selection pressure makes for cultural diversity. For a simple example, look around you at how people dress. Seasonal climatic change means a shift in the consequences of dressing lightly or heavily, so you rarely see someone wearing shorts in a New England winter or someone wearing a down parka in the summer heat and humidity. It makes little difference, however, whether you wear yellow or red or blue. This produces a lot of diversity in how people dress lightly or heavily. Employment cultures, party cultures, and some school cultures often come with more significant consequences for departures from dress norms. Offices, parties, and parochial schools generally exhibit relative uniformity in dress. The absence of consequences for dress variations in public school cultures, by contrast, creates much dress variation. Because not wearing clothes brings with it significant consequences everywhere outside of nudist camps, however, everyone wears clothes.

What Makes Consequences Change?

Change in the consequences of alternative choices produces cultural evolution. The most important events that change consequences include climate change, population change, and the human exercise of power. All current information, for example, tells us that climate change in the form of the increasingly dry conditions that followed the last ice ages created circumstances that induced the agricultural revolution. Later wetter conditions provided the basis for the rise of civilizations in Mesopotamia, Egypt, the Indus Valley, Crete, and Greece, all of which collapsed with the return of much drier conditions. In the Americas, wet conditions allowed for the development of Mayan civilization on the Yucatan Peninsula and the Mochica and Tiwanaku civilizations in the coastal and highland regions of west-central South America. All collapsed with the onset of long-term dry conditions. More recent work on the Angkor civilization of Southeast Asia tells the same story.

Population processes change consequences when fertility, mortality, or migration rises or falls, changes population density or composition, and produces either population growth or decline. Population growth meant that early farmers chose to move to find productive land or chose to assert and fight over land rights, which initiated behavioral changes that led to the emergence of patrilineal descent groups. It also induced evolution in agricultural technologies, from simple rain-fed swidden cultivation to forms of bush fallow agricultural practice to increasingly intensive and productive forms of irrigated agriculture. In China, it made profitable efforts to find rice that ripened in 60 days rather than 100, and shortly thereafter rice that ripened in 50 days rather than 60. The same field could then produce two or three crops a year rather than only one.

High population density made civilizations possible. Full-time retail traders cannot exist unless they can sell to a large number of people. The growth of a potential market of specialists makes agricultural intensification profitable. You can't erect monumental forms of architecture without lots of labor. Larger populations made for effective forms of defense against enemies and a more effective way to expand a small state into a huge empire. African economic development and technical change has been severely impeded because of low population density. Population growth reduces the supply of specific resources but it makes feasible the exploitation of others, as when coal substituted for wood in the centuries prior to the Industrial Revolution in Europe.

Teotihuacan collapsed about the same time as the Maya. The successful replacement of Teotihuacanos by the Aztecs may owe much to their development of *chinampas*. *Chinampas* are small agricultural islands constructed by building alternating layers of mud and vegetation to a level of a few inches over the level of the shallow lakes in the Valley of Mexico. The dry conditions that led to the collapse of Mayan civilization and Teotihuacan transformed what had been a single lake (Texcoco) in the Basin of Mexico into a series of five very shallow lakes. The people who lived in the Basin of Mexico worked out of natural islands and peninsulas to build these agricultural islands and planted *huejote* trees along the edge to hold the soil. They dug and maintained drainage ditches and constructed large dikes to regulate water distribution and restrict flooding. The result was a form of agriculture with extraordinarily high productivity because *chinampas* could be cropped continuously by the use of separate seed beds, irrigation from natural seepage and hand watering, and regular replenishment of their naturally high nutrient content. *Chinampas* thus require tremendous amounts of work to construct and maintain. High population density under dry conditions makes the effort worthwhile.

By changing the consequences of behavior, variation in climate or population, or both, induces changes in the assumptions we make about how best to survive, eat well reliably, and reproduce. Tightly woven baskets with which to carry seeds, or *chinampas*, may be the short-run outcomes. Because we build on the past, however, long-run outcomes have included agricultural colleges and international agricultural institutes that develop new seed varieties, preserve plant germ lines, create new means of crop production, and run extension services to pass new knowledge along to farmers. One outcome was that, between 1950 and 1980, when the world's population grew 1.9% annually, a rate faster than any we have known, the world's food supply rose still faster. Sharp declines in population, either through migration or death, meant the collapse of ancient civilizations and, in the case of the Black Death, the collapse of the English manorial system. The elimination of somewhere between one-third to one-half of the English population in the late 14th and early 15th centuries left land vacant and created significant labor shortages. Real wage levels rose dramatically and manorial dependents (*villeins*) deserted their villages or did not pay their rents. Over the previous 100 years, the rise of food prices had increased the value of agricultural land and induced the development an active market in land and tenancies among smallholding freemen and *villeins*. This helped spread the assumption that private property constituted a natural right in English culture. The rise of real wages and the growth of a population of wage earners made this right even more important, which made it a basic step in the development of free markets, which, between 1780 and 1830, initiated the industrial free-market revolution.

Cultural Evolution Shifts Course when Consequences Change

Cultures shape the behavior and ideas of the people born into them in powerful ways. But cultures don't consist of static things. They consist of things that change. They change radically when consequences change radically. This produces a clear correspondence between historical changes in the costs of consequences and changes in the prevailing cultures. The U.S. Agency for International Development (USAID) through the Institute for Development Research asked me to address this question nearly 20 years ago, although they didn't put the question in quite those words. USAID officials thought that much of the poor growth performance of African economies was explained by a shortage of indigenous entrepreneurs and limited entrepreneurial capacities among those who do exist. The absence of entrepreneurship, they supposed, must reflect intrinsic features of African culture. The few who existed came mainly from a few ethnic groups, like the Kikuyu in Kenya, the Bamileke in Cameroon, or the Hausa, Ijebu, and Igbo in Nigeria. This raised a question of how the cultures of these entrepreneurial groups differed from those of most Africans.

To address this question, I reviewed an exhaustive set of entrepreneurship cases in the private, commercial sector of contemporary African economies carried out by Africans over the last two hundred years. The report I produced in 1990 showed that Africa is brimming with entrepreneurs, that entrepreneurship emerges as part of a community culture whenever the opportunities appear, and that entrepreneurship disappears when the opportunities disappear. Changes in the consequences of options produced by the human exercise of power, in fact, explains why some ethnic groups appeared to produce entrepreneurs disproportionately: Power relationships channeled people into different life trajectories and thus dictated the extensiveness, nature and qualities of experience they acquired. The preponderance of Kikuyu entrepreneurs in Kenya, for example, owes much to the facts that they were surrounded by white settlers, constrained in territory by adjacent indigenous groups, and, although they received the greatest early exposure to Westernized forms of education, they could not use this resource to further themselves in many ways other than through entrepreneurship. Likewise, Ijebu middlemen came to dominate trade in southwestern Nigeria because they were located strategically between the coast and the interior, and they had little access to means for cash crop production or for entrance into administrative or clerical positions. Over time, increasing numbers of Ijebu youth were trained for business activities, and the development of a network of business links among Ijebu businessmen worked to strengthen the position of Ijebu entrepreneurship.

Similarly, over the course of the 20th century, Hausa created closed corporate communities in Ibadan and other Yoruba cities that facilitated business expansion and control of a variety of forms of commerce. Like the Kikuyu and Ijebu, Hausa originally entered trade because they possessed strategic economic and geographical advantages. The major cities of the Hausa emirates in northern Nigeria had been important commercial centers for centuries, coordinating trade across the Sahara and into the forested regions to the south. One part of this commerce had been a trade in cattle which were raised by Fulani in the northern savanna directed toward the Yoruba cities in the southern forests where tsetse infestations prevented cattle production in commercial quantities. European contact provided trading opportunities for Yoruba like the Ijebu who were oriented toward the coast. Hausa who had contacts with suppliers in the northern savannas emigrated to Yoruba cities to develop market outlets. By the middle of the century, Hausa landlords in Ibadan utilized a widely spread network of social relations incorporating breeders, dealers, middlemen, brokers, financiers, speculators, drovers, and scores of other intermediaries in different communities ranging from the savanna, where the Fulani raised their cattle, to the southern forest belt, where the beef was finally consumed. Many of these clients were fostered sons, for whom the landlords who controlled the trade provided marriage payments, a place to live, training, and a job.

Hausa success was due to political developments and political organization. Hausa emigrants were set apart from the Yoruba by a distinctive language and way of life. The Hausa population in Ibadan grew with the growth of commerce and, as their businesses grew, the larger Hausa landlords tried to remain free of restrictions imposed by Yoruba chiefs. They were successful perhaps mainly because Yoruba chiefs chose to deal with increasing conflicts between the two ethnic groups by isolating Hausa from the Yoruba majority. A distinct town quarter, which was called Sabo, was assigned to the Hausa, and Hausa chiefs were appointed to maintain control over ethnic Hausa.

Yoruba interlopers threatened Hausa control over trade in the 1940s. The fortuitous adoption of the Tijaniyya Order of Islam provided the vehicle of community unity in the face of these economic threats, and Hausa successfully resisted these early attempts to make inroads into the cattle trade. They also expanded their participation in other forms of commerce, most notably the trade in kola, which was grown in the southern forests and consumed in large quantities throughout the northern savanna. They even organized the begging industry. Alms-giving is one of the five pillars of Islam and begging is an honorable occupation. As the Hausa population in Ibadan grew, the lame, the blind, and lepers each eventually were assigned a chief who provided free shelter and clothing when it was necessary, and who assigned beggars to particular business sites (to which places of work they might ride back and forth in a taxi), thus providing them an income comparable to other ordinary trades. The "chiefs of the beggars" also helped coordinate a regional network of beggars that was spread throughout Yorubaland; although each town had a local core group of permanent residents, many beggars were mobile and shifted from location to location depending on the season and other factors that affected the carrying capacity of the industry.

Despite earlier Hausa successes, Yoruba butchers eventually took over the distributing functions in the cattle trade that had been monopolized by Hausa. Ibadan grew in both population and territory over the century, and Hausa butchers were not able to keep up with the increased demand, for they and their businesses were clustered in Sabo. Distribution to retailers required extensive contacts with Yoruba individuals and with market authorities and called for credit arrangements that Hausa had difficulty meeting. Perhaps most importantly, however, emigration of additional butchers from the north was discouraged because the all-Yoruba City Council made butchering subject to city regulations and licensing and gave licenses solely to Yoruba.

Over the late 19th and early 20th centuries, colonial officials and both expatriate and African traders reduced access costs to expanding world markets for cocoa, coffee, and peanuts, and agricultural entrepreneurship in West Africa achieved significant levels as early as the late 19th century. African farmers who sold to African middlemen made the Gold Coast the world's largest producer of cocoa. Cocoa exports reached 50,000 tons in 1914, 200,000 tons in the 1920s, and 300,000 tons in the 1930s. African farmers selling, initially, to African middlemen, made Senegal one of the world's leading producers of peanuts. Peanut exports Senegal reached 21,000 tons by 1870 and rose to about 600,000 tons by the 1936/1937 season. Côte d'Ivoire is an exception; there, colonial attempts to initiate coffee and cocoa production ran into severe labor shortages that the French resolved by means of demands for forced labor, which was made available to French planters, not Africans, and which was not abolished until after World War II. A significant group of African planters eventually emerged in Côte d'Ivoire, helped by infrastructural development, extension services, and buying agencies provided by government, but without credit from state or private banks, which served only French planters. Labor recruitment based on attractive terms rather than coercion transformed cocoa and coffee production. There were approximately 40,000 Ivorian cocoa and coffee producers in 1944. This figure rose to 120,000 in 1956 and to 550,000 in 1974. Cocoa and coffee exports rose from about 65,000 tons in 1945 to 160,000 tons in 1955 to a production level of 678,000 tons in 1975.

Agricultural entrepreneurship in the white settler regions of East and Central Africa, by contrast, was systematically blocked by government actions or flatly declared illegal. By the late 1920s, 20% of Kenya's arable land (nearly all of the land that was judged to have the highest productive capacity) had been confiscated and allocated to white settlers; Africans who remained on their own land were defined as "squatters" and became tenants who owed labor to Europeans. Railways, including uneconomic lines, were disproportionately concentrated in settler areas; the same was true for roads. There was a graduated pricing policy that raised freight costs for Africans and lowered them for Europeans. Europeans could receive low interest loans; Africans could not. Veterinary, medical, and farm extension services were available to European farmers; they were not available to African farmers. The public revenues spent on these services came disproportionately from Africans in the form of native and poll taxes and high customs duties on cheap articles (e.g., textiles) for the African trade; there was no income tax.

Colonial policy in Kenya, as in Côte d'Ivoire, shifted after World War II and made commercial agriculture accessible to Africans in ways that it had never been earlier in the century. Agricultural output in the Kenyan native reserves grew nearly five-fold between 1945 and 1955. Soon after independence, the new Kenyan-controlled government used a variety of loan, licensing, and public investment policies to help its constituents, many of whom were former teachers and clerks, move more effectively into commercial agriculture, trading, tourism, transportation, banking, and manufacturing. By 1977, approximately 95% of the mixed farm areas in the White Highlands that formerly had been controlled by expatriates had been taken over by Kenyans, 57% of large foreign-owned estates had been purchased by Kenyans, and over 60% of the equity in the manufacturing sector was held by Kenyans. One-quarter of the private banks in the country are now owned by Kenyans. The most effective measures were those that gave citizens preferential access to credit and business licenses, the latter of which has been the principal tool used to replace Asian with Kenyan ownership of firms in the distribution sector of the economy.

Commercial production of coffee on small plots was encouraged in Tanganyika until the mid-1920s. In the 1930s, however, the colonial government deliberately destroyed these firms and replaced them with state-controlled cooperative societies.

Agricultural entrepreneurship among black South Africans was possible in the 19th century. There, an expanding European market, information from European farmers, and deliberate missionary attempts to encourage commercial production yielded marked growth after 1830. Several thousand such farmers were to be found in the cape by the 1890s, and smaller numbers had farms in Natal and elsewhere. Some of these entrepreneurs had expanded to significant levels, owning over 3,000 acres of land, 200 cattle, and large numbers of smaller stock. Whites forcibly, albeit "legally" as based on new legislation, appropriated their land and destroyed these farms by the 1920s. Political constraints have continued to suppress entrepreneurship among black South Africans, although modest numbers of small- to middle-sized trading and service firms have existed for more than a century in the regions to which Blacks have been restricted. The number of these firms has been primarily a function of the level of effective demand for the services they offer, to which they have been restricted by law. Some black industrial entrepreneurs have emerged, although their number remains small and the scope of their firms remains highly constrained by government regulation.

Like in Kenya, the white minority in Southern Rhodesia, now Zimbabwe, forcibly appropriated nearly all of the prime agricultural land. However, agricultural entrepreneurship was actively encouraged in the Native Purchase Areas from the 1930s on. Political economic advantages granted white farmers and constraints on the growth potential of black farmers meant slow growth among the latter. By 1975, there were only about 1,000 black African farmers who had farms that averaged about 1,000 acres. After the formation of Zimbabwe in 1980, policy changes created new opportunities for black farmers; in 1986, approximately 300 Blacks engaged in large-scale commercial farming on a par with white farmers, and some 8,500 more engaged in smaller scale commercial farming using holdings that ranged from 50 to 200 hectares.

African merchants in West Africa competed very effectively with European firms during the 19th century in a trade that, by European accounts, was fiercely competitive and yielded low profit margins. More than 200 African merchants were active along the Gold Coast alone. Of these, perhaps twenty-five ran large firms—some that focused solely on the coastal import/export trade, but some that also controlled impressive interior operations, including retail stores, warehouses, and branch outlets. These firms had large payrolls that included laborers, clerks, bookkeepers, branch store managers, and traveling buyers. Some firms shipped directly to manufacturers in Great Britain and Germany. These entrepreneurs invested in land, houses, and loans, but they also pioneered new ventures, including photography studios, machine repair shops, soap manufacturing, commercial food production, newspaper publishing, gold mining, palm and rubber processing, and sawmill operations and timber exports. A combination of government action and changes in the nature of world commerce led to the failure of nearly all of these firms. The large European firms had access to resources that African firms did not: (1) larger quantities of working capital to hold large stocks in transit for long periods of time, to deal with the long interval of time between purchases from farmers and sales to manufacturers, to finance a growing network of collecting points and warehouses, and to engage in futures speculation by securing crop pledges; and (2) direct and easy access to the shippers, manufacturers, suppliers, and buyers of African products, and lower costs of operation (including freight discounts which were not offered to African merchants). Road and railway construction allowed European firms to bypass African intermediaries. The costs of production remained high in Africa when they were declining in Europe.

European and African firms in West Africa were joined by firms run by Lebanese as early as the mid-1800s. The Lebanese brought with them little money and few salable skills. Farming, factory and office work, and government employment was closed; petty trade was a viable option, although there was stiff competition from the large European merchant houses and African intermediaries. The Lebanese created a competitive advantage by accepting levels of poverty that Europeans found unacceptable and by moving into the interior. They created a reliable clientele by giving credit and adapting social reciprocities to commercial ends. Over the course of the late 19th and early 20th centuries, they thus diverted the retail trade from European-run outlets and purchased produce that otherwise would not have moved into marketing channels. They also undercut African middlemen, who generally had access to more lucrative outlets for their creative energies (notably, food and cash crop production, and government employment) and who refused, consequently, to accept the poverty that the Lebanese had no choice but to accept.

Asians faced similar conditions in East and Central Africa, with much the same result. Asian immigrants found employment in European firms more commonly than did the Lebanese in West Africa, but, outside Tanganyika, they rarely could get access to land to engage in commercial agriculture. However, colonial governments encouraged Asians to become merchants. In Northern Rhodesia (now, Zambia), Africans were not allowed to operate stores outside of African locations, could only sell goods that Europeans did not, and could not register their companies on their own land. In Uganda, African farmers increased the amount of land that they devoted to cotton from about 25,000 acres to 617,000 acres between 1910 and 1925, prodded by tax levies for those who did not plant cotton. But government licensing acts eliminated Africans from trading or ginning cotton. In Kenya, the marketing of coffee was restricted by law to Europeans and Asians. Marketing monopolies were given to Asian firms; there were statutory limits on the amount of credit that non-African firms could give to African firms.

The characteristic three-tiered trade (import and national wholesale functions carried on by European firms, middle-level wholesale and retail functions carried on by Lebanese and Asian firms, and small-scale retail functions carried on by Africans) clearly emerged only during the Great Depression when the large European firms contracted the scale of their retail operations, engaged in market sharing, and demanded (and received) government preferences in import licenses. By the mid-1930s, the top four firms on the Gold Coast controlled 70% of all exports; the top thirteen controlled about 90%. By the late 1940s, six or seven firms handled somewhere between two-thirds to three-fourths of all import/export activity. Banks charged Africans higher fees for services, frequently refused to give loans to Africans, and required forms of collateral that Africans did not have. Government gave contracts based on "past performance," which effectively excluded African entrepreneurs.

Selected Bibliography

Calvin, W. (2002). Rediscovery and the cognitive aspects of toolmaking: Lessons from the handaxe. *Behavioral and Brain Sciences*, 25, 403–404.

Cannon, W. (1970). *Bodily changes in pain, hunger, fear and rage: An account of recent researches into the function of emotional excitement.* College Park, MD: McGrath Publishing Company.

deMenocal, P.B. (2001). Cultural responses to climate change during the late Holocene. *Science*, 292, 667–673.

Handwerker, W.P. (1990). *Social dimensions of entrepreneurship in Africa.* Binghamton, NY: Institute for Development of Anthropology.

MacNeish, R.S. (1964). Ancient Mesoamerican civilization. *Science*, 143, 538–545.

The Origin of Cultures

MacNeish, R.S. (1978). The science of archaeology? *American Antiquity*, 44, 852–853.

Plutchik, R. (1980). *Theories of emotion.* New York: Academic Press.

Selye, H. (1956). *The stress of life.* New York: McGraw-Hill.

Stone, R. (2006). The end of Angkor. *Science*, 311, 1364–1368.

Weiss, H. & Bradley, R. (2001). What drives societal collapse? *Science*, 291, 609–610.

Wozniak, D.F. (Forthcoming Article). Rites of passage and healing efficacy: an ethnographic study of an intimate partner violence intervention *Journal of Global Public Health*. Published online as DOI number (10.1080/17441690902815488).

Consequences Depend on the Distribution of Power

In 1922, one of the founders of contemporary social science, Max Weber, wrote that power consists of the ability to influence or control the behavior and beliefs of others even without their consent. In this sense, the variations in climate, population, and human behavior that alter consequences exercise power. Power comes from the capacity to inflict evolutionarily significant consequences quickly and certainly. The capacity to inflict these consequences accrues to any individual, thing, or climatic or population event or process that you or I must go through to achieve goals like survival, eating well reliably, and reproducing. Variations in climate, population, and human behavior thus (to be precise) don't change cultures. They may, however, change the consequences of the choices we make. Cultures evolve in response to shifts in those consequences because they alter the behavior our minds tell us to perform.

Because colonial governments made it almost impossible for African entrepreneurs to run profitable businesses but paid their African civil servants relatively high salaries (for Africans), for example, since early in the 20th century Africa's best and brightest opted for civil service employment rather than entrepreneurship. Moreover, public sector employment made it easier to get capital for the low-level entrepreneurial functions governments left open to Africans. African entrepreneurs proliferated where and when profitable opportunities arose, namely when infrastructural development lowered the costs of access and government regulations did not unduly raise the costs of access—notably, in food production and distribution, transportation, small shops, petty trade, wood carving and metalworking for the tourist trade, and service industries like newspapers, photography, cinemas, hotels, and eating and drinking establishments.

Of these, the domestic market for food stimulated the greatest entrepreneurial development. For example, prior to European rule the Plateau Tonga of Northern Rhodesia (now, Zambia) functioned as middlemen in an extensive interregional trade in Central Africa. The imposition of colonial rule introduced expatriate traders who could provide nearly all of the traditional items of trade, often higher quality goods, at lower prices. This created a large number of unemployed Tonga traders who shifted their entrepreneurial talents to adopt new farm technologies, which they used to meet an expanding domestic market for food. Similarly, rice was introduced to the Nyakyusa of southern Tanzania, a population of perhaps 175,000 whose staple crop was bananas, just before the turn of the century. Nyakyusa adopted new agricultural methods and used savings from work on nearby coffee or tea estates, or at the Lupa goldfields (and, later, in the mines of South Africa and the Copperbelt), to acquire land and ox-plows. By 1932, rice not only had supplanted bananas as the staple food, a surplus of some 500 tons produced on the alluvial flood plains around the northern tip of Lake Nyasa was being exported from the region. Rice exports reached 1,500 tons by 1940, averaged close to 3,000 tons through the 1940s, and rose to nearly 6,000 tons by the mid-1950s.

The domestic food market grew prodigiously throughout the continent as migrants flocked to towns and cities. To serve this growing market of urban residents connected through new transportation links, the old market systems of West Africa expanded and changed their functions, and efficient marketplace distribution systems grew up where they did not previously exist in Sierra Leone and Liberia along the Windward Coast and through much of Eastern and Central Africa. Periodic markets served retailing and wholesaling or collecting functions in rural areas. Daily markets of different sizes served retailing and wholesaling functions in urban centers. Marketplaces came to exist alongside a host of itinerant petty traders and different kinds of fixed-premises firms (shops and stores) that fulfilled complementary distribution functions for imports (both food and hard goods) as well as for domestically produced foods.

The Origin of Cultures

Consequences Elicit Cultural Assumptions

Cultures exercise power because to survive, eat well reliably, and reproduce, you must negotiate your way through the behavior of other people that reflects and responds to a specific shared set of assumptions and norms. Power grows with the importance of the resources involved and the number of clients. The force exerted on our choices equals the difference in consequences between choice options with regard to their severity, certainty, and immediacy. Specific patterns of interpersonal interactions thus reflect the social distribution of power and specific assumptions and cultural norms consistent with that distribution. The concentration of power in specific people or institutions implies a corresponding reduction of evolutionarily significant consequences for the powerful and a corresponding increase of evolutionary significant consequences for others. The cultures that result work like the one described in "The Parable of the Good Son," which I wrote to summarize findings of a study of agricultural institutions in the Republic of Liberia (Handwerker 1987):

Once upon a time there were three brothers by the same father and mother. They were born and reared in a farm village in the interior of Africa and were very close. They went through school together, moved to a large city and shared lodging and, in their first jobs, all went to work for the same public agency. Here is how they differed.

One brother enjoyed his job and worked hard, resisting all temptations to use his position to enrich himself. He was dedicated to the development of his country and, being a productive worker, he rose to be manager of a department of the Ministry of Finance.

The second brother also enjoyed his work and worked hard. In his first position, agricultural extension aide, he found that several head of cattle and hogs died soon after they were delivered for him to distribute to farmers. He gave one cow to his supervisor to show gratitude for being hired as an aide and used the proceeds of the sale of the remaining meat to build a large house in his village. His parents moved into the house and rented out some of the rooms. When he was in charge of automobile procurement, he wrote two off on the official books as being beyond repair; he made one his own and sold the other to buy land near his village. When he was managing a division of the agricultural extension service, he discovered that some improved rice seed had spoiled and that several hundred rubber and coffee seedlings had been broken. Since he had shipped an earlier lot of cocoa seedlings to the farm of his Director, he planted these seeds and seedlings on his own farm. Because he could neither oversee the farm himself nor perform all the work, he appointed a cousin to manage it and hired people in the village to work on it. Soon afterwards he was arrested for embezzlement but was pardoned because of his meritorious past service. In less than a year, he was appointed Assistant Minister for Development Planning. In this position, he used his influence to make expense-paid trips abroad, to sign vouchers sent him by the Deputy Minister, and to build a large, new house in the capital city. He brought brothers, sisters, and cousins to live with him, and he sent them to school. Later, he obtained government scholarships for them to attend college or to obtain postgraduate training abroad.

The third brother looked at his job as a path to wealth. Like the second brother, the third used his position to enrich himself, but he sought only money, which he used to party, to drink, and to clothe and pay rent for girlfriends. He rose to be Assistant Controller but eventually was dismissed for embezzlement. Unlike the second brother, this third brother spent some time in jail and never again rose to so high a position.

After many years had passed, all three sons found time to visit their home village together. This was the first visit that the first and third brothers had made to their home since soon after leaving for the city. The first son was greeted cordially but sadly by his father; though he liked this son, the father thought him a fool for not taking advantage of his important position to help himself, his family, and his friends. His mother, aunt, and uncle, however, greeted him warmly, for they were proud of his accomplishments. The third son was greeted coldly by his father and mother. He was ridiculed for being a fool and for embarrassing his family and friends. The third son was told to leave the village and never return. After the villagers drove the third son from the town, they ignored the first son and killed a cow to honor the second. Only the aunt, who thought the latter a thief, did not attend the celebration.

Merit was rewarded. (pp. 307–308)

The colonial period in Africa saw the creation of state political structures designed to administer rather than to serve and, via government controlled price-fixing, monopolies, and wage and labor markets, appropriated to themselves control over the resources of the emerging world industrial system. Newly independent African governments merely took over the single-channel resource structure that had been created by the colonial powers. This created a new set of African chiefs with immense power, restricted the expansion of individual freedoms, and stressed the importance of properly managing personal relationships with the powerful, not technical competence.

In this sense, postcolonial African nations function today very much like the United States did under Andrew Jackson, when it, too, was characterized by the concentration of power into a single channel resource structure. According to Transparency International, a nongovernmental organization devoted to the eradication of corruption, a version of the Parable of the Good Son applies globally, except in Western Europe and North America. Russia ranks with Sierra Leone and Niger; Venezuela ranks with the Congo and Kyrgyzstan; Gaza and the West Bank rank with Ukraine, Zimbabwe, and the Gambia; and Haiti, Bangladesh, and Chad epitomize the worst.

Over a period of more than 200 years, by contrast, Westerners have grown up in an environment that has offered a consistently increasing number of channels by which they could secure their material well-being. The fact that there have been an increasing number of such channels has meant, generally, that they have been competitive, which has permitted an extraordinary expansion of individual freedoms, and has stressed the importance of individual technical competence. These transformative processes can occur rapidly, as experience elsewhere on the globe has revealed. Notable exceptions to corruption found worldwide include Barbados, Israel, the United Arab Emirates, Oman, Singapore, Hong Kong, Taiwan, Japan, and Chile. But these processes are only beginning to occur in Africa and elsewhere, where people grow up in an environment in which their material welfare is vitally dependent on the creation and efficient management of a selected personal network of family members and friends.

Even when these practices do not destroy the national economy, they introduce tremendous inefficiencies that slow growth and make real development a pipe dream. The largest multinationals may be able to simply ignore or bulldoze government graft and corruption because of the immense size of the investments they can make. Small and middle-sized multinationals cannot, however. African entrepreneurs suffer the most. The single-channel resource structure that characterizes modern African states has created a regulatory environment that not only requires many direct contacts with government officials, but that also systematically discriminates against small firms and operates in terms of unwritten rules that change every time a civil servant or office holder changes his or (rarely) her clientage network and every time new appointments are made. Capital and labor market policies close off opportunities to small firms and, for firms of all sizes, information costs are extraordinarily high in both time and money. Even in the best of circumstances, consequently, entrepreneurs recognize that valuable clientage ties to the public sector may evaporate without notice. This environment makes it that much more imperative to maintain a clientage network that is as diverse as possible. Ties to family members and friends outside the public sector retain an importance that they would not otherwise have. This environment also makes quick profits and diversification a far more important goal than sustained growth of a single firm based on long-term investments.

Women have suffered the most in this new configuration of power and resource access. The vast majority of African women are poorly educated and have been restricted to the tiniest forms of trade (market sellers, street sellers) and production (beer brewing, subsistence food production). Changes in power relationships thus have marginalized African women. Their importance as producers of children on whom their husbands were dependent gave African women a relatively high status in the precolonial period. Men are still dependent on their children (although less on the direct support that children can offer than on the indirect support available through clientship links to important patrons). But their control over access to schooling and jobs has given them power over women that they did not possess earlier in the century. Consequently, even women who have created significant business enterprises have had to rely heavily on husbands and lovers for business contacts, experience, hard currency, and other forms of assistance.

A Fish Rots from the Head (Kru Proverb)

The truth in Lord Acton's dictum that "power corrupts, and absolute power corrupts absolutely" is widely recognized. What I first heard as a Kru proverb I later heard described as a Russian proverb, a Chinese proverb, or one from Sicily, Greece, or somewhere else. Classic experiments both confirm and clarify the impulse for people whose choices elicit no evolutionarily significant consequences to do evil one way or another. Stanley Milgram's 1961experiment at Yale University in New Haven, Connecticut, studied what he thought of as obedience. A decade later, Phillip Zimbardo carried out a related experiment at Stanford University in Palo Alto, California, to study the effect of imprisonment on guards and prisoners. Both solicited a range of mentally stable and otherwise ordinary volunteer participants who were randomly assigned as "teachers" and "learners" in New Haven and as "guards" and "prisoners" in Palo Alto.

In New Haven, learners were strapped into what Milgram described as an electric chair apparatus to make it impossible for the learner to escape making a choice, an electrode was applied to the learner's wrist, and paste was applied to avoid blisters and burns. The experimenter explained to the accomplice learner that the shocks might be extremely painful, but that they caused no permanent damage. The experimenter and the teacher then went to a room that contained a shock generator. The shock generator had 30 voltage levels, arranged in sets of four 15-volt increments, and one set of two at the highest end. These ranged from a set labeled Slight Shock (15–60 volt level) to a set labeled Danger: Severe Shock (375–420 volt levels). The last two levels (435 and 350 volts) were labeled simply XXX. The teacher gave the learner a word pair association task. The teacher read a series of word pairs to the learner. Then the teacher read the first word of one of the pairs together with all four of the original paired items. The learner reported which of the four items correctly paired with the single word by pressing one of four switches in front of him. The answer appeared as one of four lights on the shock generator. The teacher was told to give the learner a shock for a wrong answer. The teacher was told to move one shock increment higher each time the learner gave a wrong answer. At the 20th shock level, the shock intensity reached 300 volts. At this point, the learner pounded loudly on the wall that separated the learner from the teacher, and ceased answering questions. The experimenter told the teacher to treat the absence of an answer as a wrong answer. Only five of the forty teachers ceased shocking their learners at this point. Only nine more ceased shocking their learners through the first level of the set labeled Danger: Severe Shock. Twenty-six teachers continued to shock their learners through the entire set of thirty voltage levels, *despite not having heard from the learner or having received any responses for the last ten sets of word pair tasks.* For all they knew, the learner died ten shocks earlier.

On a quiet Sunday in Palo Alto, local police went to the homes of some of the experimental volunteers, arrested them, charged them with Armed Robbery & Burglary, booked them into jail, and transported them blindfolded into the "Stanford County Jail" for further processing. Prisoners—a randomly selected set of the volunteers—were stripped, deloused, given smocks with prison ID numbers for their body (no underwear) and stocking caps for their heads, had chains placed around their ankles, and locked in small cells. Guards—a randomly selected set of the volunteers—were dressed in khaki uniforms, wore whistles around their necks, carried night sticks, and wore dark glasses. Guards were told that it was their job to maintain order and that it was dangerous to do so but important nonetheless, but were not told how. Prisoners rebelled the second day by ripping off their prison IDs, removing their stocking caps, and barricading themselves in their cells. The guards responded with anger. They sprayed prisoners with CO_2 fire extinguishers to force them back from cell doors, entered the cells, stripped the prisoners, removed the beds, isolated the ringleaders, and intensified their harassment and intimidation by denying prisoners food and washing privileges. The guards created a "privilege" cell but manipulated who was assigned to it to create distrust among the prisoners. Privileged cell members had their clothing and beds returned, received special food, and were able to wash and

The Origin of Cultures

brush their teeth. Guards increased their surveillance of prisoners and asserted control over increasing dimensions of life. Going to the toilet became a privilege that guards could deny at will, for example. At night, prisoners were increasingly likely to be required to urinate and defecate into a bucket in their cell, which they might not be allowed to empty. Acute emotional disturbances and disorganized cognition appeared among prisoners less than 3 days into the study. Guards more and more often imposed arbitrary and increasingly longer punishments, including pushups, jumping jacks, and bare hand cleaning of toilets. Around one-third of the guards appeared to genuinely enjoy intentionally sadistic behavior. The increasingly brutal behavior of guards led to the termination of the experiment by day six.

Milgram interpreted his findings as evidence of the power of authorities to command obedience. Zimbardo was struck by the quickness with which his guards dehumanized their prisoners. Parables from around the world, however, anticipated the behavior of both the teachers and the guards. Both had been placed in a position of unchecked power relative to learners and prisoners and their behavior elicited no evolutionarily significant adverse consequences. Moreover, the job of the guards was framed in a way that a lack of order among prisoners meant danger to them.

R.J. Rummel observes in his book *Death by Government* (1994) and related publications that the absolute corruption which emerges from absolute power frighteningly often shows itself as mass murder. All states murder their citizens, at least occasionally. But "death by government" occurs most often and most dramatically in the presence of highly concentrated power. The worst examples include China under Mao (who murdered an average of 2.03 million people *per year* between 1949 and 1987), the Soviet Union under Josef Stalin (who murdered an average of 1.79 million people *per year* between 1929 and 1953), Germany under Adolf Hitler (who murdered an average of 1.75 million people *per year* between 1933 and 1945), and the Pakistani army under General Agha Khan (who murdered more than 1.5 million people in what today is Bangladesh during 1971). The thirty or so lesser instances of murder by governments in recent times—in Cambodia under Pol Pot (2 million murders in 4 years), the Congo under Leopold II of Belgium (10 million murders in around 23 years), Uganda under

Idi Amin (perhaps 500,000 murders in around 8 years), for example—consistently occurred in circumstances in which power had become highly concentrated in a small group if not a single individual.

Lower Level Power Concentrations Also Unleash Violence

In Barbados and Antigua, resource structure was oligarchic before 1965. Sugar and cotton production dominated the Antiguan economy; sugar dominated Barbados's. A small number of employers controlled the private sector, so they were not subject to significant levels of competition. Consistent employment and advancement opportunities, especially prestigious civil service or bank positions, were conditional on personal contacts and personal recommendations. These, in turn, were conditional on sex, class, and color, roughly in that order of importance. In these sharply stratified and mostly lower class societies, women constituted an underclass. Men's choices dictated the opportunities available for their partners and daughters. Women's job opportunities consisted almost solely of menial employment at wages much lower than men's. Some women became teachers, nurses, or clerks. Most worked as domestic servants, seamstresses, hucksters, road gang workers, or laborers in the sugar or cotton fields.

Barbadian and Antiguan gender relations thus were predicated on women's dependence on men and their children for access to resources. Men were both gatekeepers and scarce. Women were resource seekers with little to exchange for material support other than their sexuality and childbearing capacities. Men exploited women's economic dependence on them to gain sex, children, domestic services, and unquestioned authority within their homes. Men battered women to enforce women's subservience. Open-handed slaps and cuffs or close-fisted hits or punches, collectively called "sharing licks" or "taking hand to she," probably are most common. Women also endure outright beatings with hands, belts, shoes, and other implements, choking, having their hair grabbed and pulled, having boiling water thrown over them, and being kicked and pummeled with stones, bottles, and other objects. Emotional battering encompasses accusatory and demeaning remarks that call into question women's intelligence, competence, and integrity. These include "You are a fucking idiot," "You are stupid,"

"Can't you ever do anything right," "You arsehole," and "[When] You have a problem, you always handle it wrong." Married women may be told "You stole my name" or "I married the wrong woman."

One woman in two was subject to at least moderate levels of physical and emotional battering by her partner; one woman in three was subject to intense, continuous abuse. One woman in four reported significant levels of physical and emotional abuse in her own childhood. In Barbados, one woman in three reported behavior constituting childhood or adolescent sexual abuse; one to two men in 100 reported sexual abuse. Homicide cases often arose from the circumstances that legitimized battering:

- the woman was not home when her partner arrived;
- dinner was not prepared on time, was prepared poorly, or was not food her partner liked;
- his clothes were not cleaned well;
- a woman questioned where a man was going or when he was returning or why he didn't return home the night before;
- a man heard a rumor that his woman went around with another man;
- a woman talked with other men or spent too much time with one; or
- he wanted sex and she did not;

Women had little recourse, other than to find shelter in the home of a female friend or relative. One woman described a beating she received where other men cheered her boyfriend on. Women counted on their sons to protect them. But parents and brothers were less reliable. A woman's parents might only say "But it's your husband!" One young man (early 20s) asked if he would defend his sister if she was getting beaten immediately responded: "It's her fucking problem!" He went on to say that brothers might defend a sister, "But the brother would have to love the sister very, very much. It would be very, very rare."

Not uncommonly, women described themselves as slaves in master-slave relationships. "Man gives the orders and women don't have choice but to carry them out," is how one woman put it. A 60-year-old man explained:

It has always been my belief that a man is the head of a house and that he should be able to make decisions without the help of a woman. I don't ask no wife nothing. When there is something to be done I do it. My wife can't come to tell me what is right or what is wrong. I am the person responsible for the house, so I make the decision without any help from any one. Too many people making decisions cause trouble in a house. You ever hear "Too many cooks spoil the broth"? Well, that is what I believe, too.

Another woman, 53, explained that "most men seem to see their women as just a thing that lives in the house with them, like a piece of furniture." A woman who had endured relationships filled more with hurt than happiness said;

At this point and time in my life the only thing that I really want from any man, husband or no husband, is some financial assistance. I will be very honest with you. I have found out that most of the qualities that women look for in a man are only present at the beginning of a relationship. It seem as though they put on a show for you so that they could get you into their bed. As soon as they have had all the fun they want they then begin to show negative traits. So [if] I tell you that at 52 years of age I am looking for things like love and understanding I will be fooling both you and myself. All I want from men now is anything material that they have to offer.

Men who loved their women intensely often did not know how to show it. A 68-year-old woman remarked that she "was the most surprised woman a few weeks back when [my man] tell me he has always admired the way I conducted my life and raised the children." He went on to explain that "when he was younger he was brought up to be a total man and not to stoop to any woman." "And indeed we did have some stormy times," she continued, "with him always wanting to be the boss, something which I can never understand. Anyway, now in our old age he has confessed to me that he has always admired my intelligence and sense of humor. When he said that to me it was as fresh as if he had said it back in the days when were young."

The Origin of Cultures

Subordinates Find Ways to Empower Themselves

Power corrupts because it elicits a sense of entitlement. Power elicits violence to avoid the loss of entitlements. No one likes poor treatment, even people without power. Research by Catherine Fuentes and me, for example, shows show that Whites, West Indians, Latinos, and Native Americans, as well as natives living as hunters and gatherers in the Russian and American Arctic and people making a living on tourist islands in the West Indies, concur on the properties of social interactions that constitute traumatic/violent and supportive/affectionate events. Indeed, people generally believe that their entitlements include the right to not be subject to violence.

As inequalities grow, the increase in violence exposure induces selection for moral clarity about behavioral boundaries. People who grow up in traumatic/violent (exploitative) cultural environments thus learn to be highly sensitive to power relations, respond quickly and strongly when others attempt to take advantage of them, and, to minimize the chance of further exploitation, search harder than others for ways to avoid dependency. These were the lessons learned by survivors of the 700 years of horrific violence in the lands adjacent to the Scots-English border—men, too often, are evil, and governments cannot be trusted to protect you but they can be trusted to destroy you if you give them a chance. Defense takes many forms, including physical or emotional withdrawal from a situation, behavior called "passive aggressive," protests, votes, speeches, lawsuits, angry and defensive words, and various forms of physical violence. As power differences grow both powerful and powerless people discount at increasing rates the risks they undertake to defend themselves. Because a shopkeeper confronted by an armed robber risks death whether or not he or she grabs a gun to stop the assailant, for example, grabbing the gun adds so little to the immediate threat that it doesn't count. These historical circumstances thus meant that migrants from the Scots-English border brought to America an individualism highly sensitive to threats to personal well-being, and fast, aggressive responses to those threats with the most effective weapons available. But defense may also include childbearing and patterns of sexual mobility that keep women's options open, not dependent on a single man.

Childbearing, for example, constitutes an investment activity for women without alternative sources of power. Historical sources on home life, childbearing, and men and women make clear that this was true for women in England through the late 1800s and for women in Antigua and Barbados prior to 1980. While men exploited women's economic dependence, women turned childbearing into a singularly effective means to escape subservience to unsatisfactory partners. Bearing children was essential for receiving help from men during a woman's youth. In middle age, grown children who supported their mother provided a means to escape dependence on unsatisfying relationships with men. Later, remittances from children made the difference between abject poverty and a reasonable, or even a comfortable old age.

This continues to be true for women in Africa, who find that childbearing, not employment, is virtually the only means that they can use either to secure their future material welfare or to establish the relatively permanent ties to men that improve their immediate material welfare. In rural areas, women work far harder than they did in the past, and for less return, because increasing levels of emigration of men whose remittances to their home villages have not made up for their absence have shifted even more of the agricultural work onto women's shoulders. Women in cities tend to be even more dependent on men than their rural peers. Schooling, jobs, and promotions are controlled by men, who systematically manipulate and exploit women for their own purposes. Women have responded by pursuing a strategy of cultivating relationships with multiple men simultaneously.

In both rural and urban areas, however, bearing children is essential for receiving assistance from men during a woman's youth. Because access to schooling is limited, this applies to nearly any woman who wants to pursue her education. Because avenues for employment and promotion are so limited and controlled by men, this applies to the few women who have completed secondary school or who have university degrees as well as to women who are illiterate. Women, for their part, usually drilled into the children not only how much they sacrificed and how hard they had to work to raise them properly, but also that their labors were that much worse because they had no companion to help them. It was easy to explain family hardships. Men were irresponsible and abusive. Understandably, grown children usually interpreted their obligations to help their parents as obligations to help their mother. Very much like the historical experience of women in England during the 19th century and women in the West Indies during the 20th century, in middle age, grown children who help support their mother provide a means to escape dependence on unsatisfying relationships with men.

A Shift in the Distribution of Power Elicits New Cultural Assumptions

Violence comes in forms that include bullying and stalking, the battering of women and children, shootings, stabbings, and assaults, and organized warfare and terror attacks. The premise that strength deters violence and weakness elicits it lies at the heart of Sun Tzu's 2,500–year-old *The Art of War*, Machiavelli's, *The Prince*, and Beccaria's *On Crimes and Punishments*, and rationalizes nearly all international, domestic, and personal violence prevention policies. One widely shared personal policy in U.S. culture holds that individuals should avoid "dangerous situations," meaning situations in which one makes oneself "vulnerable" because they send a signal of weakness to potential predators. It follows, and we tell children, to stay away from strangers and not to talk with them or get in their car. We tell women not to go out alone. We urge them to avoid distractions while they're out (talking on cell phones, searching purse), to walk with authority and purpose (don't look scared), if approached, to look the person in the eyes (to signal alertness), to talk with the person (to signal that you can identify them), and, if attacked, to yell, (threaten to) fight back, and to carry (something) with which to fight back effectively.

The Industrial Revolution empowered the daughters of women in Antigua and Barbados who a generation earlier lived in "dangerous situations" at home. Growth in the world economy spurred by the Industrial Revolution was marked by increasing numbers of resource access channels. Large numbers of resource access channels imply high levels of competition. High levels of both international and regional competition give selective advantages to technical skills and competences and reduce power differentials between gatekeepers and resource seekers. Opportunities for women to escape dependence on men and childbearing increased dramatically after the mid-1960s as the Antiguan economy underwent a structural change marked by a shift from an agriculturally based economy to one based primarily on tourism. The economic well-being of the emerging tourist and manufacturing sectors in Antigua and Barbados were subject to selection on the basis of quality and cost factors set in international markets. Consequently, employment and upward mobility in these sectors, and in sectors supporting manufacturing and tourism, came to be subject to selection on the basis of performance rather than personal relationships with employers. Gender, skin color, and ethnicity became progressively less important determinants of social position. Women stayed in school longer and used their education to find jobs with wages and working conditions vastly better than those available to their mothers and grandmothers.

By the 1980s, Antiguan and Barbadian women controlled their own lives in ways that had been denied their mothers and grandmothers. Children no longer served effectively as resource access channels. Children thus became consumer durables—albeit very special ones—and bearing children became a consumption activity in which parents had to choose between children or television sets and videos. Because parents have special obligations to their children—once they are born—that can and do take precedence over many (and perhaps all) other consumer choices, it became morally wrong for *bearing* children to take precedence over a woman's personal goals and dreams. The high fertility levels of midcentury were replaced by below replacement fertility by the 1980s. Moral obligations to mothers that used to be taken for granted—"giving was like breathing'" an older woman observed—became a major source of conflict between mothers who believed that their children should support them and children who believed that they owed their mothers nothing. It also became a major source of conflict among adult siblings, who began to quarrel about who should help support their mother, and in what amounts.

Women empowered by the conjunction of good job opportunities and increased educational attainment ushered in a revolution in gender relations. Both Antiguan and Barbadian women have also come to look on their relationships with men in ways significantly different from their mothers. Increasing numbers of Antiguan and Barbadian women now set agendas to which men must respond. A woman in her late 30s summarized: "Today women are more independent and won't put up with all that [abuse]. Men aren't worth the effort." Another pointed out:

> In the past, women were dependent on the men. "If you quarrel, you settle it. Now, a wife can say 'I work for myself' and just walk away. They [women] don't have much patience now. [In the past,] today we get vexed, tonight we have to sleep in the same bed. Now the woman just sleeps elsewhere.

Empowered women experience far more domestic help, emotional support, and affectionate behavior than women who are not—and little or no family violence. Women freed from dependency on childbearing had fewer children. Women simultaneously freed from dependency on men enjoyed markedly better relationships with their partners. The incidence of family violence on both Antigua and Barbados fell dramatically in just one generation. Figure 5.1 shows the replacement of a culture of violence with a culture of affection in Barbados (Box 5.1 explains how I created that figure).

Men still batter women because some women remain powerless relative to men. But whereas one in three described mothers subject to significant or intense physical and emotional abuse, less than one in ten described intense levels of abuse. In sum, relationships between Antiguan and Barbadian men and women have changed markedly. Daughters whose mothers endured openly abusive relationships offset by little affection now enjoy relationships that are only mildly abusive and that are offset by significant levels of affectionate and supportive behavior. Some women continue to defer to men. As one woman said, "All they want is a man and a wedding ring." More often, Barbadian women, like Barbadian men, have become more discriminating. A 39-year-old woman who endured 14 years of battering before she decided that "God did not mean for life to be this way," wants someone who wants to know her and is willing to put in all the time and attention it takes to do that.

A 25-year-old man expressed the new gender relations consensus concisely: "I want a partner and a friend, someone I can trust." The assumptions that men and women make about what counts as a mate and their associated norms have changed dramatically. Both men and

Figure 5.1: Cultural Transformation in Barbados

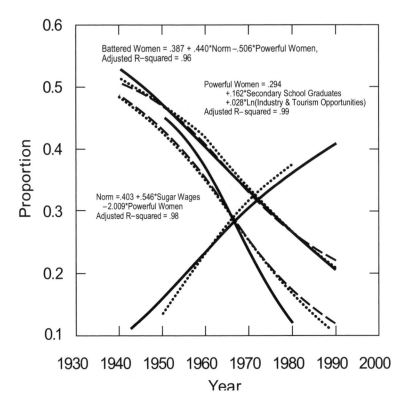

Battered Women = .387 + .440*Norm –.506*Powerful Women,
Adjusted R–squared = .96

Powerful Women = .294
+.162*Secondary School Graduates
+.028*Ln(Industry & Tourism Opportunities)
Adjusted R–squared = .99

Norm =.403 +.546*Sugar Wages
–2.009*Powerful Women
Adjusted R–squared = .98

women commonly describe hugging, touching, and sleeping wrapped around each other, or touching. A 38-year-old man pointed out that his woman "never goes to sleep at night without kissing me lightly on my lips. Sometimes during the night I feel her hand wrapped around me. Even when I am angry with her, she touch and hug me."

A 33-year-old man explained that hugging and kissing was "a daily thing": "When you love someone, that is what you do. We play all the time. It keeps me fresh and alive. Without those loving moments life would be pure hell. When I hear people saying that their men or women are not loving I wonder how they go on living with them." A 35-year-old woman pointed out that "My children's father and I have been together for a long time and I can truly say that he has never said an unkind word to me." A 46-year-old woman noted that she and her husband came to an agreement even before they were married

The Origin of Cultures

that they would always be considerate of the other and never make decisions without the other's approval. She said that this was true for something as simple as what to eat. "Whoever is doing the cooking consults the other on what to cook"—where consulting, much less cooking, was almost unheard of a generation earlier.

A 28-year-old man talked about doing things with his partner:

I am the cook of the family, but despite that when I am in the kitchen I want my girlfriend there with me. It is a lot more enjoyable when she is helping. I help her if she washes [the dishes]. I rinse and hang out. It has become automatic for us to help each other do the chores. We watch TV together, we take walks together, and go shopping together.

A 37-year-old explained:

My wife and I are involved in a business venture. We make mahogany ornaments to sell. But that got a little too small for us, so we moved into buying old mahogany furniture, refurbishing it, and selling it. We have grown now into a very big business. We also do things like sports. Actually, my wife is my friend and buddy. If I am going to cricket, she is there. If I'm jogging, she is there. She does gardening as a hobby, and now I have found myself involved in that also. It is quite empty when I have to do anything without her being along. I feel stronger when we work together.

A 43-year-old woman described her relationship this way:

He treats me more like his friend. On evening when he returns from work he is like a child seeing his mother after a long time away from home. He takes the time to talk with me and tell me all about what had taken place during the day at work. If he has a problem with any person or anything he comes to me with it. He asks my opinions and he takes my advice.

Men and women talk together, thrash out issues together, play together, and do things together in ways almost unheard of a generation earlier. Women enjoy respect and equity that did not formerly exist. A 29-year-old woman pointed out:

In my mother's time, women were taught to be seen and not heard; they knew that they were not equal to the men. They were supposed to be barefoot, pregnant and in the kitchen. [But] I consider myself as being equal with my husband. When I have somewhere to go I do not to go to him and ask if I can go; he doesn't tell me I cannot go or ask where I am going. That is left to me to decide. If I am going to tell him we have a baby, when I go out, he baby sits. My husband has lots of women calling him and I have men calling me. If he have [sic] a lover I do not know because he is very discreet about it. He does not try to embarrass me in any way.

There is companionship, too. Men teach their partners how to scuba dive and drive cars. In the evenings, they may attend language classes together after having exercised together, jogging, walking, or bicycling around the Garrison race track. Boyfriends or husbands buy their partners sewing machines to start dressmaker businesses; sell their cars to purchase a van so their partner can earn money selling cooked food at construction sites; or encourage their partner to get advanced training to be a nurse, paying the necessary university and travel fees. Men and women go into business together. The partner of a builder may come to handle the payroll and deliveries.

A 27-year-old man expressed the growing consensus when he said plainly: "A woman is not my property. If we can't agree, we part. Women are made for loving, not beating."

A 35-year-old man perhaps best explained the emerging rationale for not battering women:

In the past, men thought they had to be the boss. To "give hand to she" was very, very common. The line of thinkin today is that that is not right. A man who boasts of it is likely to be looked down on by his peers. It is one thing to scrap with another man and beat him, but women can't beat a man. It proves nothing about your manhood.

For both state and individual actors, weakness thus elicits predation and strength deters it.

BOX 5.1 What a Cultural Transformation Looks Like

Dual inheritance theorists (see Chapter 1) have developed a series of "cultural transmission"/diffusion models to study cultural transformations. The human line of evolution, however, seems to employ a cumulatively constructed learning mechanism that: (1) creatively learns from all sources of sensory information; (2) allows important innovations to spread quickly, from whatever origin; and (3) allows individuals to take advantage of innovations produced much earlier that retain their importance. They thus enhance individuals' self-reflection and self-reaction. Cultural change from whatever source, cumulative or not, may reflect the operation of three key parameters of the things that constitute choice alternatives: (1) their specific sensory properties; (2) their consequences in specific cultural environments; and (3) the source of information about the thing. Cultural change that comes solely from individuals whose minds assess choice alternatives by reference to emotional valences attached to the thing itself, the source of information about the thing, and the behavioral consequences of one thing or another thus should exhibit properties that conform to the following model:

$$p_{t+1} = p + (p^*q^*(R^*(S+C)))(1)$$

Where:

p_{t+1} = the proportion of people at the next time period who exhibit C1;

p = the proportion of people at the current time period who exhibit the new cultural form Cn;

$q = 1-p$, the proportion of people at the current time period who exhibit the old cultural form Co;

R = the Reputation coefficient (see Chapter 3);

S = the Selection coefficient (see Chapter 4);

C = the Culture coefficient (see Chapter 4).

I call the positive or negative emotional valences attached to the sensory properties of a thing their Selection coefficient. The Selection coefficient measures the difference between the relative advantage of the new (Cn) cultural form over the old (Co), independent of the effect of cultural norms and behavioral patterns A Selection coefficient of

.90 would mean that a novel cultural form produces striking improvement in a person's material well-being. I call the positive or negative emotional valences attached to the behavioral consequences of a thing their Cultural coefficient. Unlike the conformist bias in dual inheritance models, the Cultural coefficient should depend on the threat or opportunity embodied in the cultural norms and behavioral patterns that form an individual's choice environment, not directly on the number of people who exhibit one or another choice alternative.

Thus, the Cultural coefficient may attain values between -1.00 and $+1.00$. A Cultural coefficient of 0.00 means that cultural norms and behavioral patterns do not influence the probability of choice alternatives, a positive value indicates support from cultural norms and behavioral patterns, and a negative value indicates disapproval based on cultural norms and behavioral patterns. Because the Selection and Cultural coefficients respond directly to threats to and opportunities for our well-being, they should modify each other directly. A Cultural coefficient of .5 would mean that people who adopt the novelty experience a significant level of cultural disapproval. In these circumstances, we would expect that few people would adopt the new cultural form, that some who did might switch back to the old one, but that most would not.

If the Cultural coefficient remained high, it might take many, many years for a new and highly promising cultural form to spread in a population. However, we might expect that initial disbelievers might modify their views after exposure to reports of real and major improvements brought about by the new cultural form. Recognition that the novelty's promise is real thus should produce historical change in the Cultural coefficient. Significant cultural disapproval might turn into at least a moderate level of cultural approval, or cultural disapproval for not adopting the novelty. I call the positive or negative emotional valences attached to the information source their Reputation coefficient. The Reputation coefficient, by contrast, should come into play as a secondary consideration, and may exhibit both negative and positive valences. Thus, it should weight the sum of the Selection and Cultural coefficients. The R coefficient may vary above and below 1.00, where a value of 1.00 indicates no effect, a value above 1.00 indicates a boost effect, and a value below 1.00 indicates a suppressive effect.

Figure 5.1 shows three sets of lines, one each for the prevalence of (a) battered women, (b) norms for battering, and (c) powerful women on Barbados. One line in each set consists of an historical time series. A second line consists of estimates of these time series based on the multiple regression equation that corresponds with each set. The third line constitutes estimates of these time series based on Equation 1. To estimate cultural change in both behavioral patterns and cultural norms, I assumed that the source of information (R) exerted no independent effect throughout the 50 years for which we have data and set the coefficient at 1.00. I assumed that the balance of the Selection and Culture coefficients varied with the historical growth in the proportion of well-educated women with good jobs and incomes, which occurred with structural change in the national economy beginning around 1950. The result, as Figure 5.1 shows, simulations based on Equation 1 correspond closely with estimates based on multiple regression and with observed variation in historical time-series of the prevalence in patterned behavior and cultural norms.

Selected Bibliography

Bauer, P.T. (1954). *West African trade: A study of competition, oligopoly & monopoly in a changing economy.* Cambridge: University Press.

Beccharia, C. (1764 [1986 translation]). *On crimes and punishments.* Indianapolis: Hackett Publishing.

Berg, E.J. (1968). Socialist ideology and marketing policy in Africa. In R. Moyer and S.C. Hollander (Eds.), *Markets and marketing in developing economies* (pp. 24–47). Homewood, IL: Richard D. Irwin, Inc.

De Martino, B., Kumaran, D., Semour, B., and Dolan. R.J. (2006) Frames, biases, and rational decision-making in the human brain. *Science* 313, 684–687.

Handwerker, W.P. (1987). Fiscal corruption and the moral economy of resource acquisition. *Research in Economic Anthropology*, 9, 307–353.

Handwerker, W.P. (1989). *Women's power and social revolution: Fertility transition in West Indies.* Newbury Park, CA: Sage.

Handwerker, W.P. (1993). Gender power differences between parents and high risk sexual behavior: AIDS/STD risk factors extend to a prior generation. *Journal of Women's Health*, 2, 301–316.

Handwerker, W.P. (1996). Power and gender: Violence and affection experienced by children in Barbados, West Indies. *Medical Anthropology*, 17, 101–128.

Handwerker, W.P. (1998). Why violence? A test of hypotheses representing three discourses on the roots of domestic violence. *Human Organization*, 57, 200–208.

Handwerker, W.P. (2001). Child abuse and the balance of power in parental relationships: An evolved domain-independent mental mechanism that accounts for behavioral variation. *American Journal of Human Biology*, 13, 679–689.

Handwerker, W.P. (2003). Traumatic stress, ecological contingency, and sexual behavior: Antecedents and consequences of sexual precociousness, sexual mobility, and childbearing in adolescence. *Ethos*, 31, 385–411.

Haney, C., Banks, C., & Zimbardo P. (1973). A study of prisoners and guards in a simulated prison. *Naval Research Review*, 1–17.

Machiavelli, N. (1950). The prince. New York: Random House.

Milgram, S. (1963). Behavioral study of obedience. *Journal of Abnormal Psychology*, 67, 371–378.

Milgram, S. (1974). *Obedience to authority: An experimental view.* New York: Harper & Row.

Rummel, R.J. (1994). *Death by government.* New Brunswick, NJ: Transaction Publishers.

Rummel, R.J. (1995). Democracy, power, genocide, and mass murder. *Journal of Conflict Resolution*, 39, 3–26.

Rummel, R.J. (1998). *Statistics of democide: Genocide and mass murder since 1900.* Berlin: LIT Verlag.

Sun Tzu, translated by L. Giles (2005). The art of war by Sun Tzu—Special Edition. El Paso: Norte Press.

Weber, M. (1946). Wirtschaft und Gesellschaft. In H.H. Gerth & C.W. Mills (Eds.), *From Max Weber: Essays in sociology* (pp. 180–197). New York: Oxford University Press.

Zimbardo, P.G., Haney, C., Banks, W.C., & Jaffe, D. (1973). The mind is a formidable jailer: A Pirandellian prison. *New York Times Magazine*, April 8, 38–60.

The Origin of Cultures

CHAPTER SIX

Lessons Learned

I n *The Wealth of Nations*, published in 1776, Adam Smith wrote:

Every species of animal naturally multiplies in proportion to the means of their subsistence, and no species can ever multiply beyond it. . . . the scantiness of subsistence can set limits to the further multiplication of the human species; and it can do so in no other way than by destroying a great part of the children which their fruitful marriages produce. (Book I, p. 89)

Thomas Malthus substituted "potential" for Smith's "actual" population size. Because population had the *capacity* to grow faster than the food supply, the difference between the potential and the actual must be a limit, called a carrying capacity, beyond which human population growth will necessarily be checked by wars, diseases, or other disasters. Charles Darwin and Alfred Wallace independently substituted all populations for human populations in the observation that populations have the capacity to produce far more offspring than can possibly survive, and they added two further ones: (1) Organisms vary and pass along these variations to their offspring, and (2) the fit between the properties of those variations and the environment determines which offspring survive to reproduce (and how successfully) and which die. At least for Darwin, the last two observations simply substituted nature for animal breeders, who purposefully selected which of their stock would be allowed to survive and reproduce. It followed, as animal breeders of the 19th century well knew, that any novelty that increased the likelihood of survival and subsequent reproduction because of its environmental fit would accumulate in the population.

Darwin's innovation revolutionized our vision of life. The contrast between a Malthusian view and a Darwinian view perhaps is clearest if we imagine a Petri dish to which we add one bacterium. From a Malthusian perspective, the bacterium becomes bacteria, all of which will ultimately die because all the resources will ultimately be consumed. From a Darwinian perspective, the bacterium becomes bacteria that, by selection, become a myriad of new species that may consume, along with uncounted other possibilities, the Petri dish itself. Darwin's vision holds that evolution emerges from an interaction between innovations and selective *criteria* that are dictated by the properties of living things. Because all forms of life on our planet share a common ancestor, all current species merely constitute the end-points of a continuous growth trajectory for the population of life forms as a whole. The history of life on Earth has revealed an infinite supply of resources over some 3 billion years, not because environmental conditions elicit specific innovations or because living things are prescient, but because selection creates relatively advantageous means for using resources. The genetic innovations that may differentiate the offspring of common parents, which selection may concentrate into different species, change the definition of what constitutes a resource or the means used to acquire resources, and creates new niches in the environment of our Earth.

So may new ideas and new forms of behavior—like those used to control fire, produce hand-axes, select seeds for their taste and productivity, or construct machines to produce cloth, drive vehicles, and harness nuclear energy. The Protestant Ethic, which prizes hard work and deferred gratification for their own sake and for the glory of God, fits comfortably with competitive markets even if it did not create capitalist economics. Islam, too, quite effectively creates new capitalist niches, as Hausa kola and cattle traders in Nigeria discovered over the late 19th and 20th centuries. In his 1972 book *Palms, Wine, and Witnesses* and related publications, David Parkin shows, similarly, that conversion to Islam made possible significant involvement in the market economy for Giriama entrepreneurs in Kenya. Conversion both improved their health and rationalized the use of "traditional" funeral expenditures to invest in support and contacts that could be used to enlarge their farms and diversify their commercial holdings while village elders continued to bankrupt themselves on funeral expenses and lost both property and power.

Darwin's formulation itself provided a model for new ideas and forms of behavior. In 1934, Karl Popper substituted knowledge for organisms to create the view that variations in our understanding of the world were subject to selection on the basis of their fit with the observations we could make of that world. Popper thus created the foundation for what we now call Evolutionary Epistemology. In 1950, Armen Alchian substituted firms for knowledge or organisms to argue that firms vary in the degree to which they maximize profit and, hence, are subject to selection by market forces. Alchian thus created the foundation, with later contributions by Milton Friedman, Gary Becker, and the New Institutionalist theorists, for the Evolutionary Theory of the Firm. In 1965, Donald Campbell created the broadest generalization of selection applied to human behavior in his chapter "Variation and Selective Retention in Socio-Cultural Evolution." In 1966, Marvin Harris invoked selection to explain the Hindu doctrine of Ahimsa, which prohibits the killing of cattle. B.F. Skinner generalized the mechanisms of selection in his 1981 *Science* article "Selection by Consequences."

Like Darwin's application of selection to explain the origins of species, these applications of selection to variations in human behavior and thought did not account for the variations on which selection might operate. Darwin had to wait for the results from Gregor Mendel's pea experiments for serious work to begin on mechanisms of biological inheritance. Homer Barnett's description of the mental processes that produced new things provides a means by which variations in ideas and behavior come into being. William Calvin's cell assembly coded firing hypothesis subject to random intrusions may describe some of the core underlying mental processes. Together, Walter Cannon's and Hans Selye's vision of stress and Robert Plutchik's hypothesis about the origins and effects of emotions provide a selection mechanism responsible for the origin of cultures through their effects on the choices made by living things.

Cultures thus evolve from an interaction between innovations and an evolved means for choosing one option over another. Human imagination produces a continuous flow of new ideas and behaviors. The materials from which we construct choice alternatives reflect constraints or the absence of constraints on the flow of information from neighbor to neighbor and from generation to generation. But specific novelties originate unexpectedly and invariably contain imperfections.

By assigning emotional weights to the consequences of behavior for a person's ability to survive and eat well reliably, our brains may exert a selective effect by identifying knowledge and reasoning imperfections. Their weighting gives precedence to one or another mode of framing choices and thus alters the values that apply to a set of choice alternatives.

A Thought Experiment

To produce patterns of change consistent with those outlined in Chapters 4 and 5, selection must favor the evolution of a mechanism that weights choice consequences (S) by the change they produce in the likelihood that an organism will avoid death, eat well reliably and, thus, optimize its reproductive success. Because individuals who don't make it through the day never make it to next year, selection must give priority to short-run success and thus must also favor a mechanism that weights the severity (S) of a consequence by its immediacy (I) and certainty (C). Consequences that do not occur immediately introduce uncertainty, measured as certainty weighted by immediacy. The evolutionary significance (ES) of a consequence thus consists of a severity metric weighted by the immediacy and uncertainty of S: $ES = S*I*(I*C)$. To simplify talking about these issues, let's assume that each variable exhibits values between 0 and 1. ES metrics over .5 thus reflect consequence severity of at least .6 and very high levels of immediacy and certainty. ES metrics over .5 thus identify consequences that may significantly decrease the likelihood that an organism will survive well if at all.

The power that an individual or organization may wield—their ability to influence or control the behavior and beliefs of others even without their consent—therefore must come from their capacity to inflict evolutionarily significant consequences on another. This capacity accrues to any individual or organization to the extent to which it serves as gatekeeper for access to means of survival and resource access for clients. Human relationships thus should exhibit dynamics that vary with the relative power of the actors. Power grows with the importance of the resources involved and the number of clients.

Imagine for a moment that each of us could survive, eat well reliably, and reproduce without help from anyone else. That means that no one would depend on anyone else. Because you and no one else could determine the consequences that would make one choice different from another, no one could force you to do anything that you didn't otherwise want. You would be free to choose any option you wanted.

Now, let's introduce new things one by one and imagine what would happen. First, let's make you dependent on someone else. Then, let's make you dependent on someone else for something really important. Then, let's increase the number of people dependent on that same person for the same thing. Then, let's increase the number of people on whom you or others are dependent.

If you needed help with only one thing—surviving, eating well reliably, reproducing—you create inequality because you introduce power into a relationship you have with someone else. The person from whom you needed help could refuse to help you. To elicit help, you'd have to act in ways that you wouldn't otherwise, if the person you asked for help demanded it. The more important the thing with which you needed help, the more power that person would have to force you to change your behavior. So, inequality comes into being with dependence and grows with the importance of the thing with which you need help.

Let's call the person on whom you depend for something a gatekeeper. What does a gatekeeper do, as a gatekeeper? The choice to help you for no return doesn't achieve important ends, like surviving, eating well reliably, or reproducing. The choice that results in receiving something that helps you survive, eat well reliably, or reproduce achieves important ends, but only if that allows gatekeepers to remain gatekeepers. Because we come with minds that signal opportunity and danger and impel us to act on the former and avoid the latter, we should expect gatekeepers to choose options that may achieve important ends and avoid options that may endanger their position as gatekeeper. Remember: Do nothing you don't have to but everything you can to improve your well-being. Expect that help from a gatekeeper will depend on providing something in return.

Let's call you and other people dependent for help on a gatekeeper "clients." What do clients do, as clients? Because we come with minds that signal opportunity and danger, you probably don't like dependence. If you can, moreover, you'll give the gatekeeper as little as you can. If you can, you'll find another gatekeeper who asks you for less in return for help. In the best of all worlds, you'll find a way to gain direct access to food with no help from anyone, and become a gatekeeper yourself. Your interaction with other gatekeepers may take the form of fair, balanced reciprocities. Depending on your power, however, your interaction with clients may verge into corruption or predation. If your new clients include your old gatekeepers, your predatory behavior may take predatory forms we call retaliation or retribution.

Now, imagine what would happen if, as a client, you had a choice between one of five different gatekeepers. The number five possesses magical qualities, which probably reflect the well-known limitations on our short-term memory. It takes time to get to know another person well enough to anticipate what he or she will do, and still more time to stay in touch well enough to reliably anticipate the other person's behavior. Cooperation, the coordination of behavior between two or more people, requires that each reliably anticipate what the others will do. It's hard enough with five people and it quickly becomes impossible beyond that. With larger numbers of people, effective cooperation and behavioral coordination ordinarily call for grouping individuals into five or so categories of activity.

With five gatekeepers to choose among, you and the other 3,000 (or 30,000, or 300,000) people dependent on those five would do best to see if one of the others will lower the costs required for help. But gatekeepers do best if they don't have to lower their charges for help. Five gatekeepers can personally acquire and maintain the knowledge about each other necessary for reliably predicting each other's behavior. Five gatekeepers thus may effectively collude to keep from lowering their individual charges. You need more gatekeepers, say 10, or 30, or 300 to make effective collusion impossible. Once the number of gatekeepers grows beyond the point at which they can reliably anticipate what each will do, one of the gatekeepers (all of whom come with minds that signal opportunity and danger) will lower their charges to attract more clients and, so, increase his or her power compared with the others. So, the power of gatekeepers remains the same when the number of gatekeepers remains small. Because competitive gatekeepers exercise power over each other, the power of a gatekeeper declines as the number of gatekeepers grows.

The Origin of Cultures

Because the power of a gatekeeper varies with the number of his or her clients, clients exert power over gatekeepers and thus count as a kind of gatekeeper. The power of clients grows as the number of gatekeepers goes up, once the number of gatekeepers exceeds a threshold point. The power of clients probably grows at an increasingly lower rate with further growth in the number of gatekeepers. It may effectively cease at some threshold point. Who counts as a gatekeeper and who counts as a client depends on the balance of power in a relationship.

Equality thus characterizes a relationship when neither social actor depends on the other for survival and resource access, or when both depend on the other equally. Mutual dependence equality is characterized by equal capacities to inflict evolutionarily significant consequences on the other. Sanctions in the form of costly punishments may have coevolved with the propensity to cooperate. The common assumption that weakness elicits violence and strength deters it thus may come from a mind evolved to respond sensitively to variations in the immediacy and certainty with which a consequence bears on life, reliable access to food, and reproductive success. When social actors can respond (tit-for-tat) with equivalent consequences, maximum survivability comes from keeping ES below .5. Selection thus favors the evolution of a mechanism that frames behavioral choices as gains and links this choice frame with an exaggerated sense of risks. Behavioral choices that focus on gains thus avoid interactions in which ES>.5. Equals consequently engage in risk aversion strategies and, in general and on balance, treat each other well. Because equals rarely violate behavior norms in significant ways, equalities produce stability in social relations.

Equality shifts to inequality as the capacity to inflict evolutionarily significant consequences on an other person emerges and grows. Powerful people maximize their survivability by maintaining or increasing their capacity to inflict evolutionarily significant consequences on others. As ES_{max} falls for one social actor, however, selection favors the evolution of a mechanism that shifts choices framed (cautiously) as gains to choices framed as losses, and links these losses to a mechanism that decreases the weight of perceived negative outcomes in direct proportion to the evolutionary significance of the choice. As ES_{max} differences grow, consequently, behavioral choice consequences become increasingly irrelevant to powerful people who develop a growing sense of entitlement. As power differences grow larger, the fair behavior that characterizes interaction between equals shifts increasingly rapidly to increasingly exploitative and eventually violent behavior.

As the ES metrics powerless people experience grow larger than .5, clients search increasingly intensively for alternative resource access channels to counter the power of gatekeepers. Inequalities thus generate instability. So long as people frame their behavioral choices as involving gains and ES remains <.5, tit-for-tat behavioral responses keep exploitative behavior within bounds. However, once ES grows beyond .5, people fear the loss of something that constitutes their (human) right and experience anger if not outrage if their entitlements are not met. As ES grows, both powerful and powerless people discount at increasing rates the risks they undertake to defend themselves. Because a shopkeeper confronted by an armed robber risks death whether or not he or she grabs a gun to stop the assailant, for example, grabbing the gun adds so little to the immediate threat that it doesn't count. Power inequalities fall as the number or importance of alternative resource access channels grows. Growth in the ES_{max} of relatively powerless people elicits nonlinear growth in powerful people's exploitative and violent behavior, which declines once the ES_{max} of formerly powerless people exceeds .5.

People Do Violence to Defend Themselves

This means that Ayat murdered Rachel as an empowering act of self-defense. So, too, the men who beat women, the Japanese fliers who bombed Pearl Harbor, the SS who carried out Hitler's genocide, and those who carried out Stalin's orders to murder some 43,000,000 Russians. The aphorism that "one person's terrorist is another person's freedom fighter" carries an important truth: Judgments depend on cultural assumptions and the cultural norms that they rationalize. Judgments vary, too, with whether they apply to people who act violently or to the thing people try to defend.

Some cultural assumptions lead to violence rationalized in the name of religion, like Ayat's murder of Rachel with which this

The Origin of Cultures

book began. The work of Richard Sosis and colleagues over the last decade consistently shows that the 19th-century social scientist Emile Durkheim correctly observed that religion provides for unusually strong social bonds. Religious cultures thus make powerful means for achieving specific ends. Change the assumptions, however, and you change the religion that rationalizes atrocity as well as its target. Sunni and Shi'a Muslims, for example, have murdered one another for nearly 1,500 years. In the name of their emperor and religious head, as another example, in late 1937 and early 1938, Shintoists (along with some Buddhists) raped and butchered some 300,000 people, men, women, children, prisoners-of-war and civilians, after they took control of China's then capital city, Nanking. In the mid-19th century, Brigham Young established a theocracy in North America's Great Basin and encouraged his followers to kill Gentiles, Latter Day Saint (LDS) apostates, and LDS faithful whose sins warranted their death. These included forty men and eight women and children on their way to California from Arkansas slaughtered in the Mountain Meadows massacre in 1857. Between 1480 and 1530 intensively (and with less intensity through 1700), the Spanish Inquisition rooted out heretics (another name for apostate) by the torture of upward of 150,000 Jews, Protestants, and Muslims, burning 5,000 of these at the stake, the imprisonment or forced conversion to Catholicism of an unknown number of others, and by driving 40,000 Jews out of Spanish territory while they suppressed Spanish Protestants. Indian Hindus currently target Indian Christians whether Protestant or Catholic. Religions kill just like guns—only if people, directed by culturally specific assumptions, pull the trigger.

Because weakness elicits predation and strength deters it, the persistence of terrorism in today's world means that many people and both state and individual actors do nothing to stop it and much to encourage it. This means, too, that violence stops only when the parties who defend themselves find that they may reliably expect to experience behavior that elicits choices framed as gains, not losses. Historically, this has meant either an overwhelming defeat of one party by the other or stalemate. This does *not* mean that you, or a nation, should show kindness to an assailant. You experience a higher chance of dying when you treat an assailant kindly than when you try to kill him (or her). The properties of interaction depend on relative equalities. How to create those equalities without overwhelming defeat or stalemate remains one of our most important challenges.

More Often Than Not, Different *Does* Mean Better

Why? Because people choose in ways that lead them collectively to do nothing they don't have to but all they can to improve their material well-being, given the consequences of choice options. By these criteria, some things work better than others. Some people perform better than others. Some cultures work better than others. Cultures, to judge from the last 300,000 years of human history, constitute resource management designs that, with varying success, provide for collective action to address specific sustainability problems. A resource management design that works well for foragers would fare badly for rice producers. A resource management design that works well for upland rice farmers spread thinly over the landscape would fare badly for dense populations dependent on wet rice production. Neither cultural design would work for pastoralists.

The industrial free market revolution of the last 300 years, by comparison, generated a self-sustaining competitive process that continues to improve the lives of people all over the planet. Gross Domestic Product for the least-developed countries, for example, grew by a factor of 8 between 1970 and 2006. In these poorest countries in the world, life expectancy at birth grew by 38% between 1960 and 2006, and the child mortality rate was nearly cut in half. By placing a premium on individual and organizational and cultural performance, competition itself has reduced constraints on the appearance of new ideas, new ways of doing things, and the spread of information about new ideas and how to put them into operation. When competence counts, skin color, gender, and religion fade to insignificance. Barriers to competition, by contrast, facilitate the concentrations of power that defeat social justice goals. We shall look back at this time in history, I suspect, and see a transition from sharply stratified to more egalitarian global and regional relationships, despite the complexities of the leveling process and exceptions at specific times and places. Different *doesn't* mean better *only* when you cannot differentiate choices based on consequences that bear on survival, food, and reproduction.

How New Things Acquire Immense Power

The power of cultures to direct the course of human affairs comes into being as an emergent property of their collective agreement. An individual innovation exerts cultural power when and to the extent that it becomes part of a collective agreement and, so, part of the environment that we ignore at our peril. The scope of the change, Schaun Wheeler observed in a Cultural Dynamics seminar, depends simply on the ratio of the people who agree to the people who don't. Innovations thus have the biggest initial impact in small groups. They exert enormous power once they become part of a collective agreement shared by a large population.

Individual innovations become part of collective agreements by various combinations of independent invention and diffusion. Some innovations acquire cultural power by virtue, primarily, of the most dramatic form of diffusion—choices imposed by gatekeepers with enormous power. Parents comprise the most common such gatekeeper. We're all familiar with the cultural institutions that parents impose on their children, which contribute to differences between the home in which you grew up and those of your friends—and maybe your cousins. Could you go on sleep-overs or see R-rated movies? Did your family reserve Friday evenings for family activities? Did you celebrate Hanukkah or Christmas, Ramadan or Lent? What brought you most praise: excellent grades or a winning athletic performance?

Innovations forced on us may become parts of national cultures. Agreement among a small number of very powerful football agents—four of the major bowl games, five major football conferences, and the football independent, Notre Dame—imposed on the institution of college football the BCS (Bowl Championship Series). However aggravating the process was and continues to be perceived by millions and millions of people who pay to see postseason college football games, the agreement among this small number of individuals about team access to the most important (and lucrative) bowl games made the BCS a fact of life for players, coaches, colleges, sports news, and sports fans.

Indeed, innovations imposed by authorities may shape national cultures in fundamental ways. Core features of contemporary Japan, for example, reflect the decisions of a single person, General Douglas

MacArthur, who directed the reconstruction of Japan after World War II. Many of these effects came through the adoption of a new constitution modeled on that of the United States, which

* transferred the ultimate authority of the state from the emperor to the people;

* relegated the emperor to a symbol of the nation without substantive power;

* assigned a popularly elected bicameral legislature (the Diet) as the highest organ of state power.

* eliminated the military and broke up the large corporations (zaibatsu) which had controlled Japan over much of 20th-century Japan;

* gave women the vote;

* authorized the formation of labor unions; and

* guaranteed fundamental individual rights of religion, speech, thought, and association.

By breaking the feudal oligarchy that had controlled pre-war Japan, these changes along with others, including extensive land reform and workshops on American management techniques for middle-managers, MacArthur created personal freedoms heretofore unknown in Japan and thus unleashed new sources of internal competition that led to the emergence of one of the most dynamic economies in the world.

Cultural changes imposed by immensely powerful authorities take place rapidly, albeit drawn out by winnowing processes. Most forms of cultural evolution, however, appear to involve small parts of gossip-based diffusion with large parts of independent invention by individuals who respond to equivalent circumstances in equivalent ways. These forms of cultural evolution often take place as one generation, raised under one set of historically—and regionally specific circumstances, replaces another, raised in another set of historically and regionally specific circumstances. The last section of Chapter 5, for example, summarized the processes by which competition-induced structural change in the national economy and growth in the numbers of powerful women in Antigua and Barbados replaced a culture of domestic violence with a culture of domestic affection.

The Origin of Cultures

J.A. Banks provides an equivalent example. In his 1981 book *Victorian Values* Banks argues that the English fertility transition began first, some time in the late Victorian period, primarily in the mid-to-upper levels of the social and economic hierarchy. An increasingly competitive world economy meant that performance became increasingly important and that entrance to a career ladder became increasingly dependent on formal education. Increasing amounts of family resources had to be expended on public school and university education to see to it that the sons of upper-middle-class parents were to maintain the social and economic position into which they had been born. Marital fertility had to be limited to achieve that goal. Women married to men who were pursuing a meritocratic career ladder found that, like their husbands, they could look forward to a financial security that middle- and upper-class women of earlier generations could not. Resource access through children was severely circumscribed. In part, this was because children had to pass through increasingly longer unproductive periods of formal schooling. In part, this was because, once they began their own careers, children began to find that personal social relationships of patronage and clientship could not be counted on to create marked improvements in their careers. Mothers' resource access through personal relationships created by their children, which is still of vital importance in much of Africa, became decreasingly important in an economy in which competence was becoming the criterion for employment and promotion.

This change in the structure of the English economy freed middle- and upper-class women from dependence for resource access on their children but did not alleviate their dependence on their husbands. However, as education became an increasingly important criterion for career and income placement and advancement, such women found that they could contribute to the career advancement of their husbands and, thus, to their own standard of living from their youth to their old age, by reducing the number of children they bore. English fertility began to fall rapidly, however, only after the turn of the century when women, like men, found that they could look forward to genuine careers, even if those careers paid much less than the ones available to men. Women in the upper and upper middle classes found that they could create careers for themselves in the professions. Women in the lower middle classes and in the working classes began to experience the structural changes that had been experienced earlier by women higher in the English social order. Their husbands' occupations began to offer career tracks and regular increases in pay. Moreover, these women found that they, too, could create careers for themselves—for example, in teaching, midwifery, and nursing. Women's employment generated a rising standard of living.

The proportion of women who worked prior to marriage increased over the early 20th century, as did the relative proportion of women in the formal work force. Marriage and childbearing came to be looked upon very differently. Marriage increasingly became a genuine option for women, not one which was mandatory for their economic well-being. In the presence of rising real incomes, women found it less necessary to work after they were married. Some women in the lower middle class and in lower levels of the social hierarchy relied solely on their husbands for support, as did most women in the upper levels of the English social hierarchy. Worker participation rates for young married women rose consistently over the 20th century nonetheless. Increasing proportions of women found that childbearing had ceased to be an investment activity. Childbearing now restricted one's ability to work, either in a factory or to pursue a career, or to secure a satisfactory level of economic well-being from one's husband's income. Childbearing ceased to be an investment activity because the character of the economy and the character of the work and its remuneration had changed profoundly and had eliminated children's gatekeeper functions for their mothers. Fertility fell because childbearing had become a consumption activity. High fertility came to adversely affect the material aspirations of parents for themselves and their children. The moral economy of childbearing and parent-child relationships changed, and fertility transition began.

What about the Future?

In these early years of the 21st century, we confront a variety of global problems that call for choices that will carry significant consequences for our quality of life, if not our survival on the planet. These include widespread terrorism, a global avian flu epidemic with the potential to kill so many people that social and political functions beyond the local community may fail, how to maintain or increase the supplies of

The Origin of Cultures

energy on which our cultures now depend, and how to respond to climate change. Terrorism in today's world (see Chapter 1) defends the right of a deity and that deity's agents to say what is best for each of us. Terrorists likely will remain with us until state actors choose to actively defend an alternative cultural assumption, like each of us knows best what's best for ourselves. By comparison with the other global issues, the "solution" to terrorism thus appears reasonably straightforward. Whereas terrorism requires a human intervention solution, too often human interventions in health, energy, or climate make things worse rather than better.

The elusiveness of effective solutions comes partly from the character of human minds, which exhibit a propensity to seek evidence for what we already believe, or to foolishly choose what we wish was true even when we have abundant contradictory information. The Earth's climate appears to be in the midst of significant change, for example, but we can't tell for sure whether the next decade will see a dramatic rise in temperature or a new ice age. At this point, as Schaun Wheeler points out (2008:300), "We have no theory that allows us to know what we need to do next, so we are left to squabble about what we just did."

The elusiveness of effective solutions also comes from change that occurs all the time, but unexpectedly and with unpredictable substance. We thus cannot now tell exactly what the problem will be, or what resources will be available, or what new things and ideas will exist that we can bring to bear on the solution. Indeed, the problem may change, or disappear, by the time we identify it precisely and work out a solution. Sometimes people produce change. One example consists of the unexpected growth in ethanol produced from corn (rather than from, say, corn *cobs*, kudzu, or switch grass), which created a world food crisis in 2008. Some changes occur without human intervention. One example consists of the mutation that unexpectedly produced UG99 (it was first found in Uganda in 1999), a wheat rust fungus now spreading rapidly in southwest Asia that threatens to devastate the region's wheat production. If things like these didn't change, we could expect that simple winnowing would produce sustainable practices, like the rice paddies in East Asia that have been intensively cultivated for more than 1,000 years. Because they do, the sustainability of human communities hinges on their ability to respond resiliently to significant change.

Sustainability problems like these arise from complexly related sets of variables at multiple scale levels and exhibit important nonlinearities. Cultural institution design may produce, exacerbate, or minimize these problems.

In his 1952 book *The Uses of the Past*, Herbert Muller points out that the assumptions that rationalize the caste system of the Indian subcontinent, for example, deny the possibility of improving a living person's circumstances. The cultural assumption of an unchangeable reality and the ideals of renunciation of life and passivity preclude actions to improve the lives of anyone. These assumptions do not produce corruption, high death rates, and low life expectancies, but "if the temporal world is illusion there is no important difference between freedom and slavery, justice and injustice" (1952:334). These assumptions give no one who belongs among their collective adherents moral superiority over another, but they inevitably produce indifference to suffering. Because they rationalize the life circumstances of people in the lowest walks of life and give all people deprived of social justice the opportunity of a better life next time around, they ensure the safety of those who occupy the highest caste ranks.

But they also produce vulnerability to unexpected change. Muller (1952:80) observes, by contrast, that:

> No drama in history is more fascinating than the rise of Yahweh. Starting out as an obscure deity of a despised people, apparently incapable of protecting them from their enemies, he nevertheless triumphed over his far more powerful rivals and eventually conquered a mighty civilization. Offhand, it is the very model of the success story—the story of a local god who made good, against terrific odds. And it is a story of character, not luck.

Yahweh succeeded, Muller argues (1952:92), because the Prophets

> evolved a more rational, responsible history than any other people had yet conceived. Instead of foisting history on Fate, they explained it by human character and conduct. The moral value of this conception of history is plain. It puts the issue squarely up to man, declaring his responsibility for good and evil.

Judaic Prophets made possible adaptable and thriving communities in the Diaspora despite the population of adherents being "scattered over the face of the earth, despised, oppressed, persecuted, exposed to a martyrdom more cruel and prolonged than another people had had to endure" (1952:94). How? Because they denounced injustice and insisted that Jews, individually and collectively, accept moral responsibility for social justice and injustice alike.

Well before the Diaspora, Jewish culture included an assumption we ordinarily ascribe to Classical Greece, that each person knows what is best for him or her. Cultural norms that follow from this assumption include that individuals should exercise sovereignty over themselves with only those constraints that people work out together as equals, and that sovereignty violations are wrong. Cultures designed around this assumption may produce the most resilient designs because they induce people to frame choices about their sovereignty (which, therefore, bear on their survival, ability to eat reliably, and reproduce) as losses. Choices framed as losses elicit discounted risks and produce solutions that were previously impossible.

First, this cultural assumption and the norms to which it leads place a premium on independent thinking and innovation. People who start from this premise give more weight to the question of "What works?" than to questions like "What should work?" or "What do I wish would work?" These cultures thus gave rise to what we now think of as rationalism and a scientific tradition. "Science," of course, constitutes a highly effective tool not only for understanding the world but also making systematic improvements in those understandings. An emphasis on the utility of an idea or practice means that people will systematically track utility and seek changes when utility declines or may decline.

Second, because it validates the cultural norm that each individual should have a say about the activities in which they take part, the cultural assumption that each of us knows what's best for ourselves also maximizes the number of people who may contribute to a problem's solution. More ideas make for better solutions.

Third, because it leads to a norm for competition, this assumption minimizes the effects of corruption and the concentrations of power that impoverish populations.

Fourth, by contrast, it may encourage the persistence and productivity of small property owners. This would yield relatively wealthy regional economies, which between 1780 and 1830, provided the foundation for the industrial free market revolution in England.

Fifth, as Victor Davis Hanson argues in his 2001 book *Carnage and Culture*, this cultural configuration produces singularly effective militaries that triumphed in the face of huge disparities in numbers. It produced better weapons in larger numbers and armies that consisted primarily of small property owners. Their commitment to battle reflected their oversight of military operations as civilians and their expectation to both actively participate in the formulation of strategy and tactics and to receive fair treatment as soldiers. Their commitment to fellow brothers-in-arms produced the discipline that gives infantry the ability to defeat any adversary and has distinguished warfare carried out by the West for more than 2,000 years. The ability to effectively defend this cultural assumption that each individual knows best for him- or herself meant that some 2,000 years after it first flowered in Greece, Quakers, Cavaliers, and Scots-English borderers could bring it to the New World. The success of MacArthur's transformation of Japan may reflect, more than any other single thing, his insistence that this assumption be written into the new Japanese constitution and that its logical implications be followed in its formulation.

Jews in the Diaspora, Greeks who fought in the Peloponnesian War, Scots-English borderers, and General Douglas MacArthur shared a collective agreement about the truth of certain things. These truths meant that each of these individuals believed that he or she should do one thing, not another. Because their behavior corresponded to these cultural norms, they took part in something bigger than any one individual. Awareness of all these things leads you to think of yourself as a part of a team. Lack of awareness means just that. You still participate in something bigger than yourself and contribute to its effects. Each team (culture) exhibits characteristic shared behavioral patterns and forms of coordinated behavior. Team members rely on specific forms of knowledge to function as effective team members. Team norms tell each member that he or she should act in ways that produce the team's characteristic behavioral patterns and forms of coordinated behavior. Team norms rest on one or a set of assumptions, which distinguish one (culture) from another. Teams, by virtue of the ways in which they force members to make some choices rather than others, thus constitute emergent phenomena that do things, accomplish goals, and produce effects.

If our species makes it through the 21st century, it will owe its success to a "resilient" culture that promotes quick mistake correction. Each of us will contribute to the evolution of this culture. The most effective contributions may come from the cultural assumption that each person knows what is best for him- or herself and two central norms that follow. First, constraints on the flow of information impede our ability to clearly identify problems we face, and to create, formulate, and apply appropriate solutions quickly. Second, competition minimizes these constraints because it devolves power and rewards competence.

Selected Bibliography

Alchian, A. (1950). Uncertainty, evolution, and economic theory. *Journal of Political Economy*, 58, 211–221.

Bagley W. Brigham Young's Culture of Violence. Conference paper, 2002. http://www.cesnur.org/2002/slc/bagley.htm

Banks, J.A. (1981). *Victorian values: Secularism and the size of families.* Boston: Routledge & Kegan Paul.

Bauer, J. & Van Tuyll, H. (2008). *Castles, battles, and bombs: How economics explains military history.* Chicago: University of Chicago Press.

Campbell, D. (1965). Variation and selective retention in socio-cultural evolution. In H.R. Barringer, G.I. Blanksten, & R.W. Mack (Eds.), *Social change in developing areas: A reinterpretation of evolutionary theory* (pp. 19–49). Cambridge, MA: Schenkman Publishing.

Chang, I. (1997). The rape of Nanking: The forgotten holocaust of World War II. New York: Penguin.

Darwin, C. (1859). *On the origin of species.* London: John Murray.

Glimcher, P.W., Dorris, M.C., & Bayer, H.M. (2005). Physiological utility theory and the neuroeconomics of choice. *Games and Economic Behavior*, 52, 213–256.

Hanson, V.D. (2001). *Carnage and culture: Landmark battles in the rise of Western power.* New York: Doubleday.

Harris, M. (1966). The cultural ecology of India's sacred cattle. *Current Anthropology*, 7, 51–59.

Henrich, J., McElreath, R., Barr, A., Ensminger, J., Barrett, C., Bolyanatz, A., Cardenas, J.C., Gurven, M., Gwako, E., Henrich, N., Lesorogol, C., Marlowe, F., Tracer, D., & Ziker, J. (2006). Costly punishment across human societies. *Science*, 312, 1767–1770.

Inoue, K. (1991). *MacArthur's Japanese constitution: A linguistic and cultural study of its making.* Chicago: University of Chicago Press.

Malthus, T.R. (1986). *Essay on the principle of population: The first edition.* London: W. Pickering.

Muller, H.J. (1952). *The uses of the past.* New York: Oxford University Press.

Nairne, J.S., Thompson, S.R., & Pandeirada, J.N.S. (2007). Adaptive memory: Survival processing enhances retention. *Journal of Experimental Psychology: Learning, Memory, and Cognition,* 33, 263–273.

Parkin D. (1972). *Palms wine and witnesses.* Menlo Park, CA, Chandler Publishing.

Popper, K. (1968 [1934]). *The logic of scientific discovery.* London: Hutchinson.

Skinner, B.F. (1981). Selection by consequences. *Science* 213, 501–504.

Smith, A. (1776). *An inquiry into the nature and causes of the wealth of nations.* Dublin: Printed for Messrs. Whitestone.

Sosis, R. & Alcorta, C. (2003). Signaling, solidarity, and the sacred: The evolution of religious behavior. *Evolutionary Anthropology* 12, 264–274.

Sosis, R. & Alcorta, C. (2008). Militants and martyrs: Evolutionary perspectives on religion and terrorism, In R. Sagarin & T. Taylor (Eds.), *Natural security: A Darwinian approach to a dangerous world* (pp. 105–124). Berkeley: University of California Press.

Wallace, A. (1858). On the tendency of varieties to depart indefinitely from the original type. (manuscript sent to Charles Darwin). *Journal of the Proceedings of the Linnean Society: Zoology,* 3, 45–62.

Wheeler, S.J. (2008). Everything we don't know about people: An argument for a justifiable, useful, and respectable social science, with illustrations from a small, central Asian country. Unpublished Ph.D. dissertation, University of Connecticut.

Index

About the Author

W. Penn Handwerker (Ph.D., Oregon, 1971), professor of anthropology at the University of Connecticut, trained as a general anthropologist with an emphasis on the intersection of biological and cultural anthropology, and has published in all five fields (applied, archaeology, biological, cultural, and linguistics) of anthropology. He conducted field research in West Africa (Liberia), the West Indies (Barbados , Antigua, and St. Lucia), the Russian Far East, and various portions of the contemporary United States (Oregon, California's North Coast, Connecticut, and Alaska). He developed new methods with which to study cultures while he studied topics that included the causes and consequences of entrepreneurship, corruption, human fertility, and both inter- and intragenerational power differences. His current research focuses on the possibility that the most effective collective action for community sustainability reflects the cultural assumption that each person knows what's best for him- or herself.